GETTING EVEN

GETTING EVEN

WOODY ALLEN

VINTAGE BOOKS
A Division of Random House
New York

FIRST VINTAGE BOOKS EDITION, August 1978
Copyright © 1966, 1967, 1968, 1969, 1970, 1971 by
Woody Allen

All the pieces in this book appeared originally in
The New Yorker except for the following: "The Discovery
and Use of the Fake Ink Blot" first appeared in *Playboy*;
"Viva Vargas!" first appeared in the *Evergreen Review*;
"A Twenties Memory" first appeared as "How I Became a
Comedian," in *Panorama, Chicago Daily News.*
"Count Dracula," "Conversations with
Helmholtz," and "Mr. Big" were published in *Getting Even* for
the first time.

Library of Congress Cataloging in Publication Data
Allen, Woody.
    Getting even.

    I. Title.
PS3551.L44G4   1978   818'.5'407   78-55510
ISBN 0-394-72640-5

Contents

GETTING EVEN

The Metterling Lists

Venal & Sons has at last published the long-awaited
first volume of Metterling's laundry lists (*The Col-
lected Laundry Lists of Hans Metterling*, Vol. I, 437
pp., plus XXXII-page introduction; indexed; $18.75),
with an erudite commentary by the noted Metterling
scholar Gunther Eisenbud. The decision to publish this
work separately, before the completion of the immense
four-volume *œuvre*, is both welcome and intelligent, for
this obdurate and sparkling book will instantly lay to
rest the unpleasant rumors that Venal & Sons, having
reaped rich rewards from the Metterling novels, play,
and notebooks, diaries, and letters, was merely in search
of continued profits from the same lode. How wrong
the whisperers have been! Indeed, the very first Metterling laundry list

LIST No. 1
6 prs. shorts
4 undershirts
6 prs. blue socks
4 blue shirts
2 white shirts
6 handkerchiefs
No Starch

serves as a perfect, near-total introduction to this trou-

bled genius, known to his contemporaries as the
"Prague Weirdo." The list was dashed off while Metterling was writing *Confessions of a Monstrous Cheese*,
that work of stunning philosophical import in which he
proved not only that Kant was wrong about the universe
but that he never picked up a check. Metterling's dis-
like of starch is typical of the period, and when this
particular bundle came back too stiff Metterling became
moody and depressed. His landlady, Frau Weiser, re-
ported to friends that "Herr Metterling keeps to his
room for days, weeping over the fact that they have
starched his shorts." Of course, Breuer has already
pointed out the relation between stiff underwear and
Metterling's constant feeling that he was being whispered about by men with jowls (*Metterling: Paranoid-
Depressive Psychosis and the Early Lists*, Zeiss Press).
This theme of a failure to follow instructions appears in
Metterling's only play, *Asthma*, when Needleman brings
the cursed tennis ball to Valhalla by mistake.

   The obvious enigma of the second list

   LIST NO. 2
   7 prs. shorts
   5 undershirts
   7 prs. black socks
   6 blue shirts
   6 handkerchiefs
      No Starch

is the seven pairs of black socks, since it has been long
known that Metterling was deeply fond of blue. Indeed,
for years the mention of any other color could send him
into a rage, and he once pushed Rilke down into some
honey because the poet said he preferred brown-eyed
women. According to Anna Freud ("Metterling's Socks
as an Expression of the Phallic Mother," *Journal of*

Psychoanalysis, Nov., 1935), his sudden shift to the more sombre legwear is related to his unhappiness over the "Bayreuth Incident." It was there, during the first act of *Tristan*, that he sneezed, blowing the toupee off one of the opera's wealthiest patrons. The audience became convulsed, but Wagner defended him with his now classic remark "Everybody sneezes." At this, Cosima Wagner burst into tears and accused Metterling of sabotaging her husband's work.

That Metterling had designs on Cosima Wagner is undoubtedly true, and we know he took her hand once in Leipzig and again, four years later, in the Ruhr Valley. In Danzig, he referred to her tibia obliquely during a rainstorm, and she thought it best not to see him again. Returning to his home in a state of exhaustion, Metterling wrote *Thoughts of a Chicken*, and dedicated the original manuscript to the Wagners. When they used it to prop up the short leg of a kitchen table, Metterling became sullen and switched to dark socks. His housekeeper pleaded with him to retain his beloved blue or at least to try brown, but Metterling cursed her, saying, "Slut! And why not Argyles, eh?"

In the third list

LIST No. 3
6 handkerchiefs
5 undershirts
8 prs. socks
3 bedsheets
2 pillowcases

linens are mentioned for the first time: Metterling had a great fondness for linens, particularly pillow-cases, which he and his sister, as children, used to put over their heads while playing ghosts, until one day he fell into a rock quarry. Metterling liked to sleep on fresh linen, and so do his fictional creations. Horst Wasserman, the impotent locksmith in *Filet of Herring*, kills for a change of sheets, and Jenny, in *The Shepherd's Finger*, is willing to go to bed with Klineman (whom she hates for rubbing butter on her mother) "if it means lying between soft sheets." It is a tragedy that the laundry never did the linens to Metterling's satisfaction, but to contend, as Pfaltz has done, that his consternation over it prevented him from finishing *Whither Thou Goest, Cretin* is absurd. Metterling enjoyed the luxury of sending his sheets out, but he was not dependent on it.

What prevented Metterling from finishing his long-planned book of poetry was an abortive romance, which figures in the "Famous Fourth" list:

LIST NO. 4
7 prs. shorts
6 handkerchiefs
6 undershirts
7 prs. black socks
   No Starch
Special One-Day Service

In 1884, Metterling met Lou Andreas-Salomé, and suddenly, we learn, he required that his laundry be done fresh daily. Actually, the two were introduced by Nietzsche, who told Lou that Metterling was either a genius or an idiot and to see if she could guess which. At that time, the special one-day service was becoming quite popular on the Continent, particularly with intellectuals, and the innovation was welcomed by Metterling. For one thing, it was prompt, and Metterling loved promptness. He was always showing up for appointments early

—sometimes several days early, so that he would have to be put up in a guest room. Lou also loved fresh shipments of laundry every day. She was like a little child in her joy, often taking Metterling for walks in the woods and there unwrapping the latest bundle. She loved his undershirts and handkerchiefs, but most of all she worshipped his shorts. She wrote Neitzsche that Metterling's shorts were the most sublime thing she had ever encountered, including *Thus Spake Zarathustra*. Nietzsche acted like a gentleman about it, but he was always jealous of Metterling's underwear and told close friends he found it "Hegelian in the extreme." Lou Salomé and Metterling parted company after the Great Treacle Famine of 1886, and while Metterling forgave Lou, she always said of him that "his mind had hospital corners."

The fifth list

> List No. 5
> 6 undershirts
> 6 shorts
> 6 handkerchiefs

had always puzzled scholars, principally because of the total absence of socks. (Indeed, Thomas Mann, writing years later, became so engrossed with the problem he wrote an entire play about it, *The Hosiery of Moses*, which he accidentally dropped down a grating.) Why did this literary giant suddenly strike socks from his weekly list? Not, as some scholars say, as a sign of his oncoming madness, although Metterling had by now adopted certain odd behavior traits. For one thing, he believed that he was either being followed or was following somebody. He told close friends of a government plot to steal his chin, and once, on holiday in Jena, he could not say anything but the word "eggplant" for four straight days. Still, these seizures were sporadic and do not account for the missing socks. Nor does his emulation of Kafka, who for a brief period of his life stopped wearing socks, out of guilt. But Eisenbud assures us that Metterling continued to wear socks. He merely stopped sending them to the laundry! And why? Because at this time in his life he acquired a new housekeeper, Frau Milner, who consented to do his socks by hand—a gesture that so moved Metterling that he left the woman his entire fortune, which consisted of a black hat and some tobacco. She also appears as Hilda in his comic allegory, *Mother Brandt's Ichor*.

Obviously, Metterling's personality had begun to fragment by 1894, if we can deduce anything from the sixth list:

LIST NO. 6
25 handkerchiefs
 1 undershirt
 5 shorts
 1 sock

and it is not surprising to learn that it was at this time he entered analysis with Freud. He had met Freud years before in Vienna, when they both attended a production of *Oedipus*, from which Freud had to be carried out in a cold sweat. Their sessions were stormy, if we are to believe Freud's notes, and Metterling was hostile. He once threatened to starch Freud's beard and often said he reminded him of his laundryman. Gradually, Metterling's unusual relationship with his father came out. (Students of Metterling are already familiar with his father, a petty official who would frequently ridicule Metterling by comparing him to a wurst.) Freud writes of a key dream Metterling described to him:

I am at a dinner party with some friends when suddenly a man walks in with a bowl of soup on a leash. He accuses my underwear of treason, and when a lady defends me her forehead falls off. I find this amusing in the dream, and laugh. Soon everyone is laughing except my laundryman, who seems stern and sits there putting porridge in his ears. My father enters, grabs the lady's forehead, and runs away with it. He races to a public square, yelling, "At last! At last! A forehead of my own! Now I won't have to rely on that stupid son of mine." This depresses me in the dream, and I am seized with an urge to kiss the Burgomaster's laundry. (Here the patient weeps and forgets the remainder of the dream.)

With insights gained from this dream, Freud was able to help Metterling, and the two became quite friendly outside of analysis, although Freud would never let Metterling get behind him.

In Volume II, it has been announced, Eisenbud will take up Lists 7–25, including the years of Metterling's "private laundress" and the pathetic misunderstanding with the Chinese on the corner.

A Look
at Organized
Crime

It is no secret that organized crime in America takes in over forty billion dollars a year. This is quite a profitable sum, especially when one considers that the Mafia spends very little for office supplies. Reliable sources indicate that the Cosa Nostra laid out no more than six thousand dollars last year for personalized stationery, and even less for staples. Furthermore, they have one secretary who does all the typing, and only three small rooms for headquarters, which they share with the Fred Persky Dance Studio.

Last year, organized crime was directly responsible for more than one hundred murders, and *mafiosi* participated indirectly in several hundred more, either by lending the killers carfare or by holding their coats. Other illicit activities engaged in by Cosa Nostra members included gambling, narcotics, prostitution, hijacking, loansharking, and the transportation of a large whitefish across the state line for immoral purposes. The tentacles of this corrupt empire even reach into the government itself. Only a few months ago, two gang lords under federal indictment spent the night at the White House, and the President slept on the sofa.

History of Organized Crime in the United States

In 1921, Thomas (The Butcher) Covello and Ciro
(The Tailor) Santucci attempted to organize disparate
ethnic groups of the underworld and thus take over Chicago. This was foiled when Albert (The Logical Posi-
tivist) Corillo assassinated Kid Lipsky by locking him in
a closet and sucking all the air out through a straw. Lipsky's brother Mendy (alias Mendy Lewis, alias Mendy
Larsen, alias Mendy Alias) avenged Lipsky's murder
by abducting Santucci's brother Gaetano (also known as
Little Tony, or Rabbi Henry Sharpstein) and returning
him several weeks later in twenty-seven separate mason
jars. This signalled the beginning of a bloodbath.

Dominick (The Herpetologist) Mione shot Lucky
Lorenzo (so nicknamed when a bomb that went off in
his hat failed to kill him) outside a bar in Chicago. In
return, Corillo and his men traced Mione to Newark
and made his head into a wind instrument. At this point,
the Vitale gang, run by Giuseppe Vitale (real name
Quincy Baedeker), made their move to take over all
bootlegging in Harlem from Irish Larry Doyle—a rack-
eteer so suspicious that he refused to let anybody in
New York ever get behind him, and walked down the
street constantly pirouetting and spinning around.
Doyle was killed when the Squillante Construction
Company decided to erect their new offices on the
bridge of his nose. Doyle's lieutenant, Little Petey (Big
Petey) Ross, now took command; he resisted the Vitale
takeover and lured Vitale to an empty midtown garage
on the pretext that a costume party was being held
there. Unsuspecting, Vitale walked into the garage
dressed as a giant mouse, and was instantly riddled with
machine-gun bullets. Out of loyalty to their slain chief,

Vitale's men immediately defected to Ross. So did Vitale's fiancée, Bea Moretti, a showgirl and star of the hit Broadway musical *Say Kaddish*, who wound up marrying Ross, although she later sued him for divorce, charging that he once spread an unpleasant ointment on her.

Fearing federal intervention, Vincent Columbraro, the Buttered Toast King, called for a truce. (Columbraro had such tight control over all buttered toast moving in and out of New Jersey that one word from him could ruin breakfast for two-thirds of the nation.) All members of the underworld were summoned to a diner in Perth Amboy, where Columbraro told them that internal warfare must stop and that from then on they had to dress decently and stop slinking around. Letters formerly signed with a black hand would in the future be signed "Best Wishes," and all territory would be divided equally, with New Jersey going to Columbraro's mother. Thus the Mafia, or Costa Nostra (literally, "my toothpaste" or "our toothpaste"), was born. Two days later, Columbraro got into a nice hot tub to take a bath and has been missing for the past forty-six years.

Mob Structure

The Cosa Nostra is structured like any government or large corporation—or group of gangsters, for that matter. At the top is the *capo di tutti capi*, or boss of all bosses. Meetings are held at his house, and he is responsible for supplying cold cuts and ice cubes. Failure to do so means instant death. (Death, incidentally, is one of the worst things that can happen to a Cosa Nostra member, and many prefer simply to pay a fine.) Under the boss of bosses are his lieutenants, each of whom runs one section of town with his "family." Mafia families do not consist of a wife and children who always go to places like the circus or on picnics. They are actually groups of rather serious men, whose main joy in life comes from seeing how long certain people can stay under the East River before they start gurgling.

Initiation into the Mafia is quite complicated. A proposed member is blindfolded and led into a dark room. Pieces of Cranshaw melon are placed in his pockets, and he is required to hop around on one foot and cry out, "Toodles! Toodles!" Next, his lower lip is pulled out and snapped back by all the members of the board, or *commissione;* some may even wish to do it twice. Following this, some oats are put on his head. If he complains, he is disqualified. If, however, he says, "Good, I like oats on my head," he is welcomed into the brotherhood. This is done by kissing him on the cheek and shaking his hand. From that moment on, he is not permitted to eat chutney, to amuse his friends by imitating a hen, or to kill anybody named Vito.

Conclusions

Organized crime is a blight on our nation. While many young Americans are lured into a career of crime by its promise of an easy life, most criminals actually must work long hours, frequently in buildings without air-conditioning. Identifying criminals is up to each of us. Usually they can be recognized by their large cufflinks and their failure to stop eating when the man sitting next to them is hit by a falling anvil. The best methods of combatting organized crime are:

1. Telling the criminals you are not at home.
2. Calling the police whenever an unusual number of men from the Sicilian Laundry Company begin singing in your foyer.

3. Wiretapping.

Wiretapping cannot be employed indiscriminately, but its effectiveness is illustrated by this transcript of a conversation between two gang bosses in the New York area whose phones had been tapped by the F.B.I.

> Anthony: Hello? Rico?
> Rico: Hello?
> Anthony: Rico?
> Rico: Hello.
> Anthony: Rico?
> Rico: I can't hear you.
> Anthony: Is that you, Rico? I can't hear you.
> Rico: What?
> Anthony: Can you hear me?
> Rico: Hello?
> Anthony: Rico?
> Rico: We have a bad connection.
> Anthony: Can you hear me?
> Rico: Hello?
> Anthony: Rico?
> Rico: Hello?
> Anthony: Operator, we have a bad connection.
> Operator: Hang up and dial again, sir.
> Rico: Hello?

Because of this evidence, Anthony (The Fish) Rotunno and Rico Panzini were convicted and are currently serving fifteen years in Sing Sing for illegal possession of Bensonhurst.

The Schmeed Memoirs

The seemingly inexhaustible spate of literature on the Third Reich continues unabated with the soon to be published memoirs of Friedrich Schmeed. Schmeed, the best-known barber in wartime Germany, provided tonsorial services for Hitler and many highly placed government and military officials. As was noted during the Nuremberg Trials, Schmeed not only seemed to be always at the right place at the right time but possessed "more than total recall," and was thus uniquely qualified to write this incisive guide to innermost Nazi Germany. Following are a few brief excerpts:

In the spring of 1940, a large Mercedes pulled up in front of my barbershop at 127 Koenigstrasse, and Hitler walked in. "I just want a light trim," he said, "and don't take too much off the top." I explained to him there would be a brief wait because von Ribbentrop was ahead of him. Hitler said he was in a rush and asked Ribbentrop if he could be taken next, but Ribbentrop insisted it would look bad for the Foreign Office if he were passed over. Hitler thereupon made a quick phone call, and Ribbentrop was immediately transferred to the Afrika Korps, and Hitler got his haircut. This sort of rivalry went on all the time. Once, Göring had Heydrich detained by the police on false pretenses, so that he could get the chair by the window. Göring was a dissolute and often wanted to sit on the hobbyhorse to get his haircuts. The Nazi high command was embarrassed by this but could do nothing. One day, Hess challenged him. "I want the hobbyhorse today, Herr Field Marshal," he said.

"Impossible. I have it reserved," Göring shot back.

"I have orders directly from the Führer. They state that I am to be allowed to sit on the horse for my haircut." And Hess produced a letter from Hitler to that effect. Göring was livid. He never forgave Hess, and said that in the future he would have his wife cut his hair at home with a bowl. Hitler laughed when he heard this, but Göring was serious and would have carried it out had not the Minister of Arms turned down his requisition for a thinning shears.

I have been asked if I was aware of the moral implications of what I was doing. As I told the tribunal at Nuremberg, I did not know that Hitler was a Nazi. The truth was that for years I thought he worked for the phone company. When I finally did find out what a monster he was, it was too late to do anything, as I had made a down payment on some furniture. Once, toward the end of the war, I did contemplate loosening the Führer's neck-napkin and allowing some tiny hairs to get down his back, but at the last minute my nerve failed me.

At Berchtesgaden one day, Hitler turned to me and said, "How would I look in sideburns?" Speer laughed, and Hitler became affronted. "I'm quite serious, Herr Speer," he said. "I think I might look good in sideburns." Göring, that obsequious clown, concurred instantly, saying, "The Führer in sideburns—what an excellent idea!" Speer still disagreed. He was, in fact, the only one with enough integrity to tell the Führer when he needed a haircut. "Too flashy," Speer said now. "Sideburns are the kind of thing I'd associate with Churchill." Hitler became incensed. Was Churchill contemplating sideburns, he wanted to know, and if so, how many and when? Himmler, supposedly in charge of Intelligence, was summoned immediately. Göring was annoyed by Speer's attitude and whispered to him, "Why are you making waves, eh? If he wants sideburns, let him have sideburns." Speer, usually tactful to a fault, called Göring a hypocrite and "an order of bean curd in a German uniform." Göring swore he would get even, and it was rumored later that he had special S.S. guards french Speer's bed.

Himmler arrived in a frenzy. He had been in the midst of a tap-dancing lesson when the phone rang, summoning him to Berchtesgaden. He was afraid it was about a misplaced carload of several thousand coneshaped party hats that had been promised Rommel for his winter offensive. (Himmler was not accustomed to being invited to dinner at Berchtesgaden, because his eyesight was poor and Hitler could not bear to watch him bring the fork up to his face and then stick the food somewhere on his cheek.) Himmler knew something was wrong, because Hitler was calling him "Shorty," which he only did when annoyed. Suddenly the Führer turned on him, shouting, "Is Churchill going to grow sideburns?"

Himmler turned red.

"Well?"

Himmler said there had been word that Churchill contemplated sideburns but it was all unofficial. As to size and number, he explained, there would probably be two, of a medium length, but no one wanted to say before they could be sure. Hitler screamed and banged his

fist on the table. (This was a triumph for Göring over
Speer.) Hitler pulled out a map and showed us how he
meant to cut off England's supply of hot towels. By
blockading the Dardanelles, Doenitz could keep the
towels from being brought ashore and laid across anxiously awaiting British faces. But the basic question remained: Could Hitler beat Churchill to sideburns?
Himmler said Churchill had a head start and that it
might be impossible to catch him. Göring, that vacuous
optimist, said the Führer could probably grow sideburns
quicker, particularly if we marshalled all of Germany's
might in a concentrated effort. Von Rundstedt, at a
meeting of the General Staff, said it was a mistake to try
to grow sideburns on two fronts at once and advised
that it would be wiser to concentrate all efforts on one
good sideburn. Hitler said he could do it on both cheeks
simultaneously. Rommel agreed with von Rundstedt.
"They will never come out even, *mein Führer*," he said.
"Not if you rush them." Hitler became enraged and said
that it was a matter for him and his barber. Speer promised he could triple our output of shaving cream by the
fall, and Hitler was euphoric. Then, in the winter of
1942, the Russians launched a counter-offensive and
the sideburns came to a halt. Hitler grew despondent,
fearing that soon Churchill would look wonderful while
he still remained "ordinary," but shortly thereafter we
received news that Churchill had abandoned the idea
of sideburns as too costly. Once again the Führer had
been proved right.

After the Allied invasion, Hitler developed dry, un-
ruly hair. This was due in part to the Allies' success and
in part to the advice of Goebbels, who told him to wash
it every day. When General Guderian heard this, he
immediately returned home from the Russian front and

told the Führer he must shampoo his hair no more than three times weekly. This was the procedure followed with great success by the General Staff in two previous wars. Hitler once again overruled his generals and continued washing daily. Bormann helped Hitler with the rinsing and always seemed to be there with a comb. Eventually, Hitler became dependent on Bormann, and before he looked in a mirror he would always have Bormann look in it first. As the Allied armies pushed east, Hitler's hair grew worse. Dry and unkempt, he often raged for hours about how he would get a nice haircut and a shave when Germany won the war, and maybe even a shine. I realize now he never had any intention of doing those things.

One day, Hess took the Führer's bottle of Vitalis and set out in a plane for England. The German high command was furious. They felt Hess planned to give it to the Allies in return for amnesty for himself. Hitler was particularly enraged when he heard the news, as he had just stepped out of the shower and was about to do his hair. (Hess later explained at Nuremberg that his plan was to give Churchill a scalp treatment in an effort to end the war. He had got as far as bending Churchill over a basin when he was apprehended.)

Late in 1944, Göring grew a mustache, causing talk that he was soon to replace Hitler. Hitler was furious and accused Göring of disloyalty. "There must be only one mustache among the leaders of the Reich, and it shall be mine!" he cried. Göring argued that two mustaches might give the German people a greater sense of hope about the war, which was going poorly, but Hitler thought not. Then, in January of 1945, a plot by several generals to shave Hitler's mustache in his sleep and proclaim Doenitz the new leader failed when von Stauffenberg, in the darkness of Hitler's bedroom, shaved off one of the Führer's eyebrows instead. A state of emergency was proclaimed, and suddenly Goebbels appeared at my shop. "An attempt was just made on the Führer's mustache; but it was unsuccessful," he said, trembling. Goebbels arranged for me to go on radio and address the German people, which I did, with a minimum of notes. "The Führer is all right," I assured them. "He still has his mustache. Repeat. The Führer still has his mustache. A plot to shave it has failed."

Near the end, I came to Hitler's bunker. The Allied armies were closing in on Berlin, and Hitler felt that if the Russians got there first he would need a full haircut but if the Americans did he could get by with a light trim. Everyone quarrelled. In the midst of all this, Bormann wanted a shave, and I promised him I would get to work on some blueprints. Hitler grew morose and remote. He talked of parting his hair from ear to ear and then claimed that the development of the electric razor would turn the war for Germany. "We will be able to shave in seconds, eh, Schmeed?" he muttered. He mentioned other wild schemes and said that someday he would have his hair not just cut but shaped. Obsessed as usual by sheer size, he vowed he would eventually have a huge pompadour—"one that will make the world tremble and will require an honor guard to comb." Finally, we shook hands and I gave him a last trim. He tipped me one pfennig. "I wish it could be more," he said, "but ever since the Allies have overrun Europe I've been a little short."

My Philosophy

The development of my philosophy came about as follows: My wife, inviting me to sample her very first soufflé, accidentally dropped a spoonful of it on my foot, fracturing several small bones. Doctors were called in, X-rays taken and examined, and I was ordered to bed for a month. During this convalescence, I turned to the works of some of Western society's most formidable thinkers—a stack of books I had laid aside for just such an eventuality. Scorning chronological order, I began with Kierkegaard and Sartre, then moved quickly to Spinoza, Hume, Kafka, and Camus. I was not bored, as I had feared I might be; rather, I found myself fascinated by the alacrity with which these great minds unflinchingly attacked morality, art, ethics, life, and death. I remember my reaction to a typically luminous observation of Kierkegaard's: "Such a relation which relates itself to its own self (that is to say, a self) must either have constituted itself or have been constituted by another." The concept brought tears to my eyes. My word, I thought, to be that clever! (I'm a man who has trouble writing two meaningful sentences on "My Day at the Zoo.") True, the passage was totally incomprehensible to me, but what of it as long as Kierkegaard was having fun? Suddenly confident that metaphysics was the work

I had always been meant to do, I took up my pen and
began at once to jot down the first of my own musings.
The work proceeded apace, and in a mere two afternoons
—with time out for dozing and trying to get the two
little BBs into the eyes of the bear—I had completed
the philosophical work that I am hoping will not be un-
covered until after my death, or until the year 3000
(whichever comes first), and which I modestly believe
will assure me a place of reverence among history's
weightiest thinkers. Here is but a small sample of the
main body of intellectual treasure that I leave for pos-
terity, or until the cleaning woman comes.

I. Critique of Pure Dread

In formulating any philosophy, the first consideration
must always be: What can we know? That is, what can
we be sure we know, or sure that we know we knew it,
if indeed it is at all knowable. Or have we simply forgotten it and are too embarrassed to say anything? Descartes hinted at the problem when he wrote, "My mind
can never know my body, although it has become quite
friendly with my legs." By "knowable," incidentally, I
do not mean that which can be known by perception of
the senses, or that which can be grasped by the mind,
but more that which can be said to be Known or to possess a Knownness or Knowability, or at least something
you can mention to a friend.

Can we actually "know" the universe? My God, it's
hard enough finding your way around in Chinatown.
The point, however, is: Is there anything out there?
And why? And must they be so noisy? Finally, there
can be no doubt that the one characteristic of "reality"
is that it lacks essence. That is not to say it has no es-

sence, but merely lacks it. (The reality I speak of here is the same one Hobbes described, but a little smaller.) Therefore the Cartesian dictum "I think, therefore I am" might be better expressed "Hey, there goes Edna with a saxophone!" So, then, to know a substance or an idea we must doubt it, and thus, doubting it, come to perceive the qualities it possesses in its finite state, which are truly "in the thing itself," or "of the thing itself," or of something or nothing. If this is clear, we can leave epistemology for the moment.

II. Eschatological Dialectics As a Means of Coping with Shingles

We can say that the universe consists of a substance, and this substance we will call "atoms," or else we will call it "monads." Democritus called it atoms. Leibnitz called it monads. Fortunately, the two men never met, or there would have been a very dull argument. These "particles" were set in motion by some cause or underlying principle, or perhaps something fell someplace. The point is that it's too late to do anything about it now, except possibly to eat plenty of raw fish. This, of course, does not explain why the soul is immortal. Nor does it say anything about an afterlife, or about the feeling my Uncle Sender has that he is being followed by Albanians. The causal relationship between the first principle (i.e., God, or a strong wind) and any teleological concept of being (Being) is, according to Pascal, "so ludicrous that it's not even funny (Funny)." Schopenhauer called this "will," but his physician diagnosed it as hay fever. In his later years, he became embittered by it, or more likely because of his increasing suspicion that he was not Mozart.

III. The Cosmos on Five Dollars a Day

What, then, is "beautiful"? The merging of harmony with the just, or the merging of harmony with something that just sounds like "the just"? Possibly harmony should have been merged with "the crust" and this is what's been giving us our trouble. Truth, to be sure, is beauty—or "the necessary." That is, what is good or possessing the qualities of "the good" results in "truth." If it doesn't, you can bet the thing is not beautiful, although it may still be waterproof. I am beginning to think I was right in the first place and that everything should be merged with the crust. Oh, well.

Two Parables

A man approaches a palace. Its only entrance is guarded by some fierce Huns who will only let men named Julius enter. The man tries to bribe the guards by offering them a year's supply of choice chicken parts. They neither scorn his offer nor accept it, but merely take his nose and twist it till it looks like a Molly screw. The man says it is imperative that he enter the palace because he is bringing the emperor a change of underwear. When the guards still refuse, the man begins to Charleston. They seem to enjoy his dancing but soon become morose over the treatment of the Navajos by the federal government. Out of breath, the man collapses. He dies, never having seen the emperor and owing the Steinway people sixty dollars on a piano he had rented from them in August.

●

I am given a message to deliver to a general. I ride and ride, but the general's headquarters seem to get farther and farther away. Finally, a giant black panther leaps upon me and devours my mind and heart. This puts a terrific crimp in my evening. No matter how hard I try, I cannot catch the general, whom I see running in the distance in his shorts and whispering the word "nutmeg" to his enemies.

Aphorisms

It is impossible to experience one's own death objectively and still carry a tune.

•

The universe is merely a fleeting idea in God's mind —a pretty uncomfortable thought, particularly if you've just made a down payment on a house.

•

Eternal nothingness is O.K. if you're dressed for it.

•

If only Dionysus were alive! Where would he eat?

•

Not only is there no God, but try getting a plumber on weekends.

Yes, But Can the Steam Engine Do This?

I was leafing through a magazine while waiting for Joseph K., my beagle, to emerge from his regular Tuesday fifty-minute hour with a Park Avenue therapist—a Jungian veterinarian who, for fifty dollars per session, labors valiantly to convince him that jowls are not a social drawback—when I came across a sentence at the bottom of the page that caught my eye like an overdraft notice. It was jut another item in one of those boiler-plate specials with a title like "Historagrams" or "Betcha Didn't Know," but its magnitude shook me with the power of the opening strains of Beethoven's Ninth. "The sandwich," it read, "was invented by the Earl of Sandwich." Stunned by the news, I read it again and broke into an involuntary tremble. My mind whirled as it began to conjure with the immense dreams, the hopes and obstacles, that must have gone into the invention of the first sandwich. My eyes became moist as I looked out the window at the shimmering towers of the city, and I experienced a sense of eternity, marvelling at man's ineradicable place in the universe. Man the inventor! Da Vinci's notebooks loomed before me—brave blueprints for the highest aspirations of the human race. I thought of Aristotle, Dante, Shakespeare. The First

Folio. Newton. Handel's *Messiah*. Monet. Impression-
ism. Edison. Cubism. Stravinsky. $E = mc^2$ . . .

Holding firmly to a mental picture of the first sandwich lying encased at the British Museum, I spent the
ensuing three months working up a brief biography of
its great inventor, his nibs the Earl. Though my grasp
of history is a bit shaky, and though my capacity for
romanticizing easily dwarfs that of the average acid-
head, I hope I have captured at least the essence of this
unappreciated genius, and that these sparse notes will
inspire a true historian to take it from here.

1718: Birth of the Earl of Sandwich to upper-class
parents. Father is delighted at being appointed chief
farrier to His Majesty the King—a position he will enjoy for several years, until he discovers he is a black-
smith and resigns embittered. Mother is a simple *Haus-
frau* of German extraction, whose uneventful menu
consists essentially of lard and gruel, although she does
show some flair for the culinary imagination in her abil-
ity to concoct a passable sillabub.

1725-35: Attends school, where he is taught horse-
back riding and Latin. At school he comes in contact
with cold cuts for the first time and displays an unusual
interest in thinly sliced strips of roast beef and ham. By
graduation this has become an obsession, and although
his paper on "The Analysis and Attendant Phenomena
of Snacks" arouses interest among the faculty, his class-
mates regard him as odd.

1736: Enters Cambridge University, at his parents'
behest, to pursue studies in rhetoric and metaphysics,
but displays little enthusiasm for either. In constant re-
volt against everything academic, he is charged with
stealing loaves of bread and performing unnatural ex-

periments with them. Accusations of heresy result in his
expulsion.

1738: Disowned, he sets out for the Scandinavian
countries, where he spends three years in intensive re-
search on cheese. He is much taken with the many va-
rieties of sardines he encounters and writes in his note-
book, "I am convinced that there is an enduring reality,
beyond anything man has yet attained, in the juxtaposi-
tion of foodstuffs. Simplify, simplify." Upon his return
to England, he meets Nell Smallbore, a greengrocer's
daughter, and they marry. She is to teach him all he
will ever know about lettuce.

1741: Living in the country on a small inheritance,
he works day and night, often skimping on meals to
save money for food. His first completed work—a slice
of bread, a slice of bread on top of that, and a slice of
turkey on top of both—fails miserably. Bitterly disappointed, he returns to his studio and begins again.

1745: After four years of frenzied labor, he is convinced he is on the threshold of success. He exhibits
before his peers two slices of turkey with a slice of
bread in the middle. His work is rejected by all but
David Hume, who senses the imminence of something
great and encourages him. Heartened by the philosopher's friendship, he returns to work with renewed
vigor.

1747: Destitute, he can no longer afford to work in
roast beef or turkey and switches to ham, which is
cheaper.

1750: In the spring, he exhibits and demonstrates
three consecutive slices of ham stacked on one another;
this arouses some interest, mostly in intellectual circles,
but the general public remains unmoved. Three slices
of bread on top of one another add to his reputation,

and while a mature style is not yet evident, he is sent for by Voltaire.

1751: Journeys to France, where the dramatist-philosopher has achieved some interesting results with bread and mayonnaise. The two men become friendly and begin a correspondence that is to end abruptly when Voltaire runs out of stamps.

1758: His growing acceptance by opinion-makers wins him a commission by the Queen to fix "something special" for a luncheon with the Spanish ambassador. He works day and night, tearing up hundreds of blueprints, but finally—at 4:17 A.M., April 27, 1758—he creates a work consisting of several strips of ham enclosed, top and bottom, by two slices of rye bread. In a burst of inspiration, he garnishes the work with mustard. It is an immediate sensation, and he is commissioned to prepare all Saturday luncheons for the remainder of the year.

1760: He follows one success with another, creating "sandwiches," as they are called in his honor, out of roast beef, chicken, tongue, and nearly every conceivable cold cut. Not content to repeat tried formulas, he seeks out new ideas and devises the combination sandwich, for which he receives the Order of the Garter.

1769: Living on a country estate, he is visited by the greatest men of his century; Haydn, Kant, Rousseau, and Ben Franklin stop at his home, some enjoying his remarkable creations at table, others ordering to go.

1778: Though aging physically he still strives for new forms and writes in his diary, "I work long into the cold nights and am toasting everything now in an effort to keep warm." Later that year, his open hot roast-beef sandwich creates a scandal with its frankness.

1783: To celebrate his sixty-fifth birthday, he invents the hamburger and tours the great capitals of the world personally, making burgers at concert halls before large and appreciative audiences. In Germany, Goethe suggests serving them on buns—an idea that delights the Earl, and of the author of *Faust* he says, "This Goethe, he is some fellow." The remark delights Goethe, although the following year they break intellectually over the concept of rare, medium, and well done.

1790: At a retrospective exhibition of his works in London, he is suddenly taken ill with chest pains and is thought to be dying, but recovers sufficiently to supervise the construction of a hero sandwich by a group of talented followers. Its unveiling in Italy causes a riot, and it remains misunderstood by all but a few critics.

1792: He develops a genu varum, which he fails to treat in time, and succumbs in his sleep. He is laid to rest in Westminster Abbey, and thousands mourn his passing. At his funeral, the great German poet Hölderlin sums up his achievements with undisguised reverence: "He freed mankind from the hot lunch. We owe him so much."

Death
Knocks

*(The play takes place in the bedroom of the Nat Acker-
mans' two-story house, somewhere in Kew Gardens.
The carpeting is wall-to-wall. There is a big double bed
and a large vanity. The room is elaborately furnished
and curtained, and on the walls there are several paint-
ings and a not really attractive barometer. Soft theme
music as the curtain rises. Nat Ackerman, a bald,
paunchy fifty-seven-year-old dress manufacturer is lying on the bed finishing off tomorrow's* Daily News. *He
wears a bathrobe and slippers, and reads by a bed light
clipped to the white headboard of the bed. The time is
near midnight. Suddenly we hear a noise, and Nat sits
up and looks at the window.)*

Nat: What the hell is that?

*(Climbing awkwardly through the window is a som-
bre, caped figure. The intruder wears a black hood and
skintight black clothes. The hood covers his head but
not his face, which is middle-aged and stark white. He
is something like Nat in appearance. He huffs audibly
and then trips over the windowsill and falls into the
room.)*

Death *(for it is no one else)*: Jesus Christ. I nearly
broke my neck.

Nat (*watching with bewilderment*): Who are you?

Death: Death.

Nat: Who?

Death: Death. Listen—can I sit down? I nearly broke my neck. I'm shaking like a leaf.

Nat: Who *are* you?

Death: *Death.* You got a glass of water?

Nat: Death? What do you mean, Death?

Death: What is wrong with you? You see the black costume and the whitened face?

Nat: Yeah.

Death: Is it Halloween?

Nat: No.

Death: Then I'm Death. Now can I get a glass of water—or a Fresca?

Nat: If this is some joke—

Death: What kind of joke? You're fifty-seven? Nat Ackerman? One-eighteen Pacific Street? Unless I blew it—where's that call sheet? (*He fumbles through pocket, finally producing a card with an address on it. It seems to check.*)

Nat: What do you want with me?

Death: What do I want? What do you think I want?

Nat: You must be kidding. I'm in perfect health.

Death (*unimpressed*): Uh-huh. (*Looking around*) This is a nice place. You do it yourself?

Nat: We had a decorator, but we worked with her.

Death (*looking at picture on the wall*): I love those kids with the big eyes.

Nat: I don't want to go yet.

Death: *You* don't want to go? Please don't start in. As it is, I'm nauseous from the climb.

Nat: What climb?

Death: I climbed up the drainpipe. I was trying to make a dramatic entrance. I see the big windows and you're awake reading. I figure it's worth a shot. I'll climb up and enter with a little—you know . . . (*Snaps fingers*) Meanwhile, I get my heel caught on some vines, the drainpipe breaks, and I'm hanging by a thread. Then my cape begins to tear. Look, let's just go. It's been a rough night.

Nat: You broke my drainpipe?

Death: Broke. It didn't break. It's a little bent. Didn't you hear anything? I slammed into the ground.

Nat: I was reading.

Death: You must have really been engrossed. (*Lifting newspaper Nat was reading*) "NAB COEDS IN POT ORGY." Can I borrow this?

Nat: I'm not finished.

Death: Er—I don't know how to put this to you, pal . . .

Nat: Why didn't you just ring downstairs?

Death: I'm telling you, I could have, but how does it look? This way I get a little drama going. Something. Did you read *Faust*?

Nat: What?

Death: And what if you had company? You're sitting there with important people. I'm Death—I should ring the bell and traipse right in the front? Where's your thinking?

Nat: Listen, Mister, it's very late.

Death: Yeah. Well, you want to go?

Nat: Go where?

Death: Death. It. The Thing. The Happy Hunting Grounds. (*Looking at his own knee*) Y'know, that's a pretty bad cut. My first job, I'm liable to get gangrene yet.

Nat: Now, wait a minute. I need time. I'm not ready to go.

Death: I'm sorry. I can't help you. I'd like to, but it's the moment.

Nat: How can it be the moment? I just merged with Modiste Originals.

Death: What's the difference, a couple of bucks more or less.

Nat: Sure, what do you care? You guys probably have all your expenses paid.

Death: You want to come along now?

Nat (*studying him*): I'm sorry, but I cannot believe you're Death.

Death: Why? What'd you expect—Rock Hudson?

Nat: No, it's not that.

Death: I'm sorry if I disappointed you.

Nat: Don't get upset. I don't know, I always thought you'd be . . . uh . . . taller.

Death: I'm five seven. It's average for my weight.

Nat: You look a little like me.

Death: Who should I look like? I'm your death.

Nat: Give me some time. Another day.

Death: I can't. What do you want me to say?

Nat: One more day. Twenty-four hours.

Death: What do you need it for? The radio said rain tomorrow.

Nat: Can't we work out something?

Death: Like what?

Nat: You play chess?

Death: No, I don't.

Nat: I once saw a picture of you playing chess.

Death: Couldn't be me, because I don't play chess. Gin rummy, maybe.

Nat: You play gin rummy?

Death: Do I play gin rummy? Is Paris a city?

Nat: You're good, huh?

Death: Very good.

Nat: I'll tell you what I'll do—

Death: Don't make any deals with me.

Nat: I'll play you gin rummy. If you win, I'll go immediately. If I win, give me some more time. A little bit —one more day.

Death: Who's got time to play gin rummy?

Nat: Come on. If you're so good.

Death: Although I feel like a game . . .

Nat: Come on. Be a sport. We'll shoot for a half hour.

Death: I really shouldn't.

Nat: I got the cards right here. Don't make a production.

Death: All right, come on. We'll play a little. It'll relax me.

Nat (*getting cards, pad, and pencil*): You won't regret this.

Death: Don't give me a sales talk. Get the cards and give me a Fresca and put out something. For God's sake, a stranger drops in, you don't have potato chips or pretzels.

Nat: There's M&M's downstairs in a dish.

Death: M&M's. What if the President came? He'd get M&M's, too?

Nat: You're not the President.

Death: Deal.

(*Nat deals, turns up a five.*)

Nat: You want to play a tenth of a cent a point to make it interesting?

Death: It's not interesting enough for you?

Nat: I play better when money's at stake.

Death: Whatever you say, Newt.

Nat: Nat. Nat Ackerman. You don't know my name?

Death: Newt, Nat—I got such a headache.

Nat: You want that five?

Death: No.

Nat: So pick.

Death (*surveying his hand as he picks*): Jesus, I got nothing here.

Nat: What's it like?

Death: What's what like?

(*Throughout the following, they pick and discard.*)

Nat: Death.

Death: What should it be like? You lay there.

Nat: Is there anything after?

Death: Aha, you're saving twos.

Nat: I'm asking. Is there anything after?

Death (*absently*): You'll see.

Nat: Oh, then I will actually see something?

Death: Well, maybe I shouldn't have put it that way. Throw.

Nat: To get an answer from you is a big deal.

Death: I'm playing cards.

Nat: All right, play, play.

Death: Meanwhile, I'm giving you one card after another.

Nat: Don't look through the discards.

Death: I'm not looking. I'm straightening them up. What was the knock card?

Nat: Four. You ready to knock already?

Death: Who said I'm ready to knock? All I asked was what was the knock card?

Nat: And all I asked was is there anything for me to look forward to.

Death: Play.

Nat: Can't you tell me anything? Where do we go?

Death: We? To tell you the truth, *you* fall in a crumpled heap on the floor.

Nat: Oh, I can't wait for that! Is it going to hurt?

Death: Be over in a second.

Nat: Terrific. (*Sighs*) I needed this. A man merges with Modiste Originals . . .

Death: How's four points?

Nat: You're knocking?

Death: Four points is good?

Nat: No, I got two.

Death: You're kidding.

Nat: No, you lose.

Death: Holy Christ, and I thought you were saving sixes.

Nat: No. Your deal. Twenty points and two boxes. Shoot. (*Death deals.*) I must fall on the floor, eh? I can't be standing over the sofa when it happens?

Death: No. Play.

Nat: Why not?

Death: Because you fall on the floor! Leave me alone. I'm trying to concentrate.

Nat: Why must it be on the floor? That's all I'm saying! Why can't the whole thing happen and I'll stand next to the sofa?

Death: I'll try my best. Now can we play?

Nat: That's all I'm saying. You remind me of Moe Lefkowitz. He's also stubborn.

Death: I remind him of Moe Lefkowitz. I'm one of the most terrifying figures you could possibly imagine, and him I remind of Moe Lefkowitz. What is he, a furrier?

Nat: You should be such a furrier. He's good for eighty thousand a year. Passementeries. He's got his own factory. Two points.

Death: What?

Nat: Two points. I'm knocking. What have you got?

Death: My hand is like a basketball score.

Nat: And it's spades.

Death: If you didn't talk so much.

(*They redeal and play on.*)

Nat: What'd you mean before when you said this was your first job?

Death: What does it sound like?

Nat: What are you telling me—that nobody ever went before?

Death: Sure they went. But I didn't take them.

Nat: So who did?

Death: Others.

Nat: There's others?

Death: Sure. Each one has his own personal way of going.

Nat: I never knew that.

Death: Why should you know? Who are you?

Nat: What do you mean who am I? Why—I'm nothing?

Death: Not nothing. You're a dress manufacturer. Where do you come to knowledge of the eternal mysteries?

Nat: What are you talking about? I make a beautiful dollar. I sent two kids through college. One is in advertising, the other's married. I got my own home. I drive a Chrysler. My wife has whatever she wants. Maids, mink coat, vacations. Right now she's at the Eden Roc. Fifty dollars a day because she wants to be near her sister. I'm supposed to join her next week, so what do you think I am—some guy off the street?

Death: All right. Don't be so touchy.

Nat: Who's touchy?

Death: How would you like it if I got insulted quickly?

Nat: Did I insult you?

Death: You didn't say you were disappointed in me?

Nat: What do you expect? You want me to throw you a block party?

Death: I'm not talking about that. I mean me person-ally. I'm too short, I'm this, I'm that.

Nat: I said you looked like me. It's like a reflection.

Death: All right, deal, deal.

(*They continue to play as music steals in and the lights dim until all is in total darkness. The lights slowly come up again, and now it is later and their game is over. Nat tallies.*)

Nat: Sixty-eight . . . one-fifty . . . Well, you lose.

Death (*dejectedly looking through the deck*): I knew I shouldn't have thrown that nine. Damn it.

Nat: So I'll see you tomorrow.

Death: What do you mean you'll see me tomorrow?

Nat: I won the extra day. Leave me alone.

Death: You were serious?

Nat: We made a deal.

Death: Yeah, but—

Nat: Don't "but" me. I won twenty-four hours. Come back tomorrow.

Death: I didn't know we were actually playing for time.

Nat: That's too bad about you. You should pay attention.

Death: Where am I going to go for twenty-four hours?

Nat: What's the difference? The main thing is I won an extra day.

Death: What do you want me to do—walk the streets?

Nat: Check into a hotel and go to a movie. Take a *schvitz*. Don't make a federal case.

Death: Add the score again.

Nat: Plus you owe me twenty-eight dollars.

Death: *What?*

Nat: That's right, Buster. Here it is—read it.

Death (*going through pockets*): I have a few singles
—not twenty-eight dollars.

Nat: I'll take a check.

Death: From what account?

Nat: Look who I'm dealing with.

Death: Sue me. Where do I keep my checking account?

Nat: All right, gimme what you got and we'll call it
square.

Death: Listen, I need that money.

Nat: Why should you need money?

Death: What are you talking about? You're going to
the Beyond.

Nat: So?

Death: So—you know how far that is?

Nat: So?

Death: So where's gas? Where's tolls?

Nat: We're going by car!

Death: You'll find out. (*Agitatedly*) Look—I'll be
back tomorrow, and you'll give me a chance to win the
money back. Otherwise I'm in definite trouble.

Nat: Anything you want. Double or nothing we'll
play. I'm liable to win an extra week or a month. The
way you play, maybe years.

Death: Meantime I'm stranded.

Nat: See you tomorrow.

Death (*being edged to the doorway*): Where's a good
hotel? What am I talking about hotel, I got no money.
I'll go sit in Bickford's. (*He picks up the* News.)

Nat: Out. Out. That's my paper. (*He takes it back.*)

Death (*exiting*): I couldn't just take him and go. I
had to get involved in rummy.

Nat (*calling after him*): And be careful going downstairs. On one of the steps the rug is loose.

(*And, on cue, we hear a terrific crash. Nat sighs, then crosses to the bedside table and makes a phone call.*)

Nat: Hello, Moe? Me. Listen, I don't know if somebody's playing a joke, or what, but Death was just here. We played a little gin . . . No, *Death*. In person. Or somebody who claims to be Death. But, Moe, he's such a *schlep!*

CURTAIN

Spring
Bulletin

The number of college bulletins and adult-education come-ons that keep turning up in my mailbox convinces me that I must be on a special mailing list for dropouts. Not that I'm complaining; there is something about a list of extension courses that piques my interest with a fascination hitherto reserved for a catalogue of Hong Kong honeymoon accessories, sent to me once by mistake. Each time I read through the latest bulletin of extension courses, I make immediate plans to drop everything and return to school. (I was ejected from college many years ago, the victim of unproved accusations not unlike those once attached to Yellow Kid Weil.) So far, however, I am still an uneducated, unextended adult, and I have fallen into the habit of browsing through an imaginary, handsomely printed course bulletin that is more or less typical of them all:

Summer Session

Economic Theory: A systematic application and critical evaluation of the basic analytic concepts of economic theory, with an emphasis on money and why it's good. Fixed coefficient production functions, cost and supply curves, and nonconvexity comprise the first semester, with the second semester concentrating on spending, making change, and keeping a neat wallet. The Federal Reserve System is analyzed, and advanced students are coached in the proper method of filling out a deposit slip. Other topics include: Inflation and Depression— how to dress for each. Loans, interest, welching.

History of European Civilization: Ever since the discovery of a fossilized eohippus in the men's washroom at Siddon's Cafeteria in East Rutherford, New Jersey, it has been suspected that at one time Europe and America were connected by a strip of land that later sank or became East Rutherford, New Jersey, or both. This throws a new perspective on the formation of European society and enables historians to conjecture about why it sprang up in an area that would have made a much better Asia. Also studied in the course is the decision to hold the Renaissance in Italy.

Introduction to Psychology: The theory of human behavior. Why some men are called "lovely individuals" and why there are others you just want to pinch. Is there a split between mind and body, and, if so, which is better to have? Aggression and rebellion are discussed. (Students particularly interested in these aspects of psychology are advised to take one of these Winter Term courses: Introduction to Hostility; Intermediate Hostility; Advanced Hatred; Theoretical Foundations of Loathing.) Special consideration is given to a study of consciousness as opposed to unconsciousness, with many helpful hints on how to remain conscious.

Psychopathology: Aimed at understanding obsessions and phobias, including the fear of being suddenly captured and stuffed with crabmeat, reluctance to return a volleyball serve, and the inability to say the word "mack-inaw" in the presence of women. The compulsion to seek out the company of beavers is analyzed.

Philosophy I: Everyone from Plato to Camus is read, and the following topics are covered:

Ethics: The categorical imperative, and six ways to make it work for you.

Aesthetics: Is art the mirror of life, or what?

Metaphysics: What happens to the soul after death? How does it manage?

Epistemology: Is knowledge knowable? If not, how do we know this?

The Absurd: Why existence is often considered silly, particularly for men who wear brown-and-white shoes. Manyness and oneness are studied as they relate to otherness. (Students achieving oneness will move ahead to twoness.)

Philosophy XXIX-B: Introduction to God. Confrontation with the Creator of the universe through informal lectures and field trips.

The New Mathematics: Standard mathematics has recently been rendered obsolete by the discovery that for years we have been writing the numeral five backward. This has led to a reëvaluation of counting as a method of getting from one to ten. Students are taught advanced concepts of Boolean Algebra, and formerly unsolvable equations are dealt with by threats of reprisals.

Fundamental Astronomy: A detailed study of the universe and its care and cleaning. The sun, which is made of gas, can explode at any moment, sending our entire planetary system hurtling to destruction; students are advised what the average citizen can do in such a case. They are also taught to identify various constellations, such as the Big Dipper, Cygnus the Swan, Sagittarius the Archer, and the twelve stars that form Lumides the Pants Salesman.

Modern Biology: How the body functions, and where it can usually be found. Blood is analyzed, and it is learned why it is the best possible thing to have coursing through one's veins. A frog is dissected by students and its digestive tract is compared with man's, with the frog giving a good account of itself except on curries.

Rapid Reading: This course will increase reading speed a little each day until the end of the term, by which time the student will be required to read *The Brothers Karamazov* in fifteen minutes. The method is to scan the page and eliminate everything except pronouns from one's field of vision. Soon the pronouns are eliminated. Gradually the student is encouraged to nap. A frog is dissected. Spring comes. People marry and die. Pinkerton does not return.

Musicology III: The Recorder. The student is taught how to play "Yankee Doodle" on this end-blown wooden flute, and progresses rapidly to the Brandenburg Concertos. Then slowly back to "Yankee Doodle."

Music Appreciation: In order to "hear" a great piece of music correctly, one must: (1) know the birthplace of the composer, (2) be able to tell a rondo from a scherzo, and back it up with action. Attitude is important. Smiling is bad form unless the composer has in-

tended the music to be funny, as in *Till Eulenspiegel*,
which abounds in musical jokes (although the trombone
has the best lines.) The ear, too, must be trained, for it
is our most easily deceived organ and can be made to
think it is a nose by bad placement of stereo speakers.
Other topics include: The four-bar rest and its potential
as a political weapon. The Gregorian Chant: Which
monks kept the beat.

Writing for the Stage: All drama is conflict. Character
development is also very important. Also what they say.
Students learn that long, dull speeches are not so effec-
tive, while short, "funny" ones seem to go over well.
Simplified audience psychology is explored: Why is a
play about a lovable old character named Gramps often
not as interesting in the theatre as staring at the back of
someone's head and trying to make him turn around?
Interesting aspects of stage history are also examined.
For example, before the invention of italics, stage directions were often mistaken for dialogue, and great
actors frequently found themselves saying, "John rises,
crosses left." This naturally led to embarrassment and,
on some occasions, dreadful notices. The phenomenon
is analyzed in detail, and students are guided in avoiding
mistakes. Required text: A. F. Shulte's *Shakespeare:
Was He Four Women?*

Introduction to Social Work: A course designed to in-
struct the social worker who is interested in going out
"in the field." Topics covered include: how to organize
street gangs into basketball teams, and vice versa; play-
grounds as a means of preventing juvenile crime, and
how to get potentially homicidal cases to try the sliding
pond; discrimination; the broken home; what to do if
you are hit with a bicycle chain.

Yeats and Hygiene, A Comparative Study: The poetry of William Butler Yeats is analyzed against a background of proper dental care. (Course open to a limited number of students.)

Hassidic Tales, with a Guide to Their Interpretation by the Noted Scholar

A man journeyed to Chelm in order to seek the advice of Rabbi Ben Kaddish, the holiest of all ninth-century rabbis and perhaps the greatest *noodge* of the medieval era.

"Rabbi," the man asked, "where can I find peace?"

The Hassid surveyed him and said, "Quick, look behind you!"

The man turned around, and Rabbi Ben Kaddish smashed him in the back of the head with a candlestick. "Is that peaceful enough for you?" he chuckled, adjusting his *yarmulke*.

In this tale, a meaningless question is asked. Not only is the question meaningless but so is the man who journeys to Chelm to ask it. Not that he was so far away from Chelm to begin with, but why shouldn't he stay where he is? Why is he bothering Rabbi Ben Kaddish—the Rabbi doesn't have enough trouble? The truth is, the Rabbi's in over his head with gamblers, and he has also been named in a paternity case by a Mrs. Hecht. No, the point of this tale is that this man has nothing better to do with his time than journey around and get on people's nerves. For this, the Rabbi bashes his head in, which, according to the Torah, is one of the most subtle methods of showing concern. In a similar version of this tale, the Rabbi leaps on top of the man in a frenzy and carves the story of Ruth on his nose with a stylus.

●

Rabbi Raditz of Poland was a very short rabbi with a long beard, who was said to have inspired many pogroms with his sense of humor. One of his disciples asked, "Who did God like better—Moses or Abraham?"

"Abraham," the Zaddik said.

"But Moses led the Israelites to the Promised Land," said the disciple.

"All right, so Moses," the Zaddik answered.

"I understand, Rabbi. It was a stupid question."

"Not only that, but you're stupid, your wife's a *meeskeit*, and if you don't get off my foot you're excommunicated."

Here the Rabbi is asked to make a value judgment between Moses and Abraham. This is not an easy matter, particularly for a man who has never read the Bible and has been faking it. And what is meant by the hopelessly relative term "better"? What is "better" to the Rabbi is not necessarily "better" to his disciple. For instance, the Rabbi likes to sleep on his stomach. The disciple also likes to sleep on the Rabbi's stomach. The problem here is obvious. It should also be noted that to step on a rabbi's foot (as the disciple does in the tale) is a sin, according to the Torah, comparable to the fondling of matzos with any intent other than eating them.

●

A man who could not marry off his ugly daughter visited Rabbi Shimmel of Cracow. "My heart is heavy," he told the Rev, "because God has given me an ugly daughter."

"How ugly?" the Seer asked.

"If she were lying on a plate with a herring, you wouldn't be able to tell the difference."

The Seer of Cracow thought for a long time and finally asked, "What kind of herring?"

The man, taken aback by the query, thought quickly and said, "Er—Bismarck."

"Too bad," the Rabbi said. "If it was Maatjes, she'd have a better chance."

Here is a tale that illustrates the tragedy of transient qualities such as beauty. Does the girl actually resemble a herring? Why not? Have you seen some of the things walking around these days, particularly at resort areas? And even if she does, are not all creatures beautiful in God's eyes? Perhaps, but if a girl looks more at home in a jar of wine sauce than in an evening gown she's got big problems. Oddly enough, Rabbi Shimmel's own wife was said to resemble a squid, but this was only in the face, and she more than made up for it by her hacking cough—the point of which escapes me.

●

Rabbi Zwi Chaim Yisroel, an Orthodox scholar of the Torah and a man who developed whining to an art unheard of in the West, was unanimously hailed as the wisest man of the Renaissance by his fellow-Hebrews, who totalled a sixteenth of one per cent of the population. Once, while he was on his way to synagogue to celebrate the sacred Jewish holiday commemorating God's reneging on every promise, a woman stopped him and asked the following question: "Rabbi, why are we not allowed to eat pork?"

"We're *not*?" the Rev said incredulously. "Uh-oh."

This is one of the few stories in all Hassidic literature that deals with Hebrew law. The Rabbi knows he shouldn't eat pork; he doesn't care, though, because he *likes* pork. Not only does he like pork; he gets a kick out of rolling Easter eggs. In short, he cares very little about traditional Orthodoxy and regards God's covenant with Abraham as "just so much chin music." Why pork was proscribed by Hebraic law is still unclear, and some scholars believe that the Torah merely suggested not eating pork at certain restaurants.

●

Rabbi Baumel, the scholar of Vitebsk, decided to embark on a fast to protest the unfair law prohibiting Russian Jews from wearing loafers outside the ghetto. For sixteen weeks, the holy man lay on a crude pallet, staring at the ceiling and refusing nourishment of any kind. His pupils feared for his life, and then one day a woman came to his bedside and, leaning down to the learned scholar, asked, "Rabbi, what color hair did Esther have?" The Rev turned weakly on his side and faced her. "Look what she picks to ask me!" he said. "You know what kind of a headache I got from sixteen weeks without a bite!" With that, the Rabbi's disciples escorted her personally into the *sukkah*, where she ate bounteously from the horn of plenty until she got the tab.

This is a subtle treatment of the problem of pride and vanity, and seems to imply that fasting is a big mistake. Particularly on an empty stomach. Man does not bring on his own unhappiness, and suffering is really God's will, although why He gets such a kick out of it is beyond me. Certain Orthodox tribes believe suffering is the only way to redeem oneself, and scholars write of a cult called the Essenes, who deliberately went around bumping into walls. God, according to the later books of Moses, is benevolent, although there are still a great many subjects he'd rather not go into.

●

Rabbi Yekel of Zans, who had the best diction in the world until a Gentile stole his resonant underwear, dreamed three nights running that if he would only journey to Vorki he would find a great treasure there. Bidding his wife and children goodbye, he set out on a trip, saying he would return in ten days. Two years later, he was found wandering the Urals and emotionally involved with a panda. Cold and starving, the Rev was taken back to his home, where he was revived with steaming soup and flanken. Following that, he was given something to eat. After dinner, he told this story: Three days out of Zans, he was set upon by wild nomads. When they learned he was a Jew, they forced him to alter all their sports jackets and take in their trousers. As if this were not humiliation enough, they put sour cream in his ears and sealed them with wax. Finally, the Rabbi escaped and headed for the nearest town, winding up in the Urals instead, because he was ashamed to ask directions.

After telling the story, the Rabbi rose and went into his bedroom to sleep, and, behold, under his pillow was the treasure that he originally sought. Ecstatic, he got down and thanked God. Three days later, he was back wandering in the Urals again, this time in a rabbit suit.

The above small masterpiece amply illustrates the absurdity of mysticism. The Rabbi dreams *three* straight nights. The Five Books of Moses subtracted from the Ten Commandments leaves five. Minus the brothers Jacob and Esau leaves *three*. It was reasoning like this that led Rabbi Yitzhok Ben Levi, the great Jewish mystic, to hit the double at Aqueduct fifty-two days running and still wind up on relief.

The Gossage — Vardebedian Papers

My Dear Vardebedian:

I was more than a bit chagrined today, on going through the morning's mail, to find that my letter of September 16, containing my twenty-second move (knight to the king's fourth square), was returned unopened due to a small error in addressing—precisely, the omission of your name and residence (how Freudian can one get?), coupled with a failure to append postage. That I have been disconcerted of late due to equivocation in the stock market is no secret, and though on the above-mentioned September 16 the culmination of a long-standing downward spiral dropped Amalgamated Anti-Matter off the Big Board once and for all, reducing my broker suddenly to the legume family, I do not offer this as an excuse for my negligence and monumental ineptitude. I goofed. Forgive me. That you failed to notice the missing letter indicates a certain disconcertion on your part, which I put down to zeal, but heaven knows we all make mistakes. That's life—and chess.

Well, then, the error laid bare, simple rectification follows. If you would be so good as to transfer my knight to your king's fourth square I think we may proceed with our little game more accurately. The announcement of checkmate which you made in this morning's mail is, I fear, in all fairness, a false alarm, and if you will reëxamine the positions in light of to-day's discovery, you will find that it is *your* king that lies close to mate, exposed and undefended, an immobile target for my predatory bishops. Ironic, the vicissitudes of miniature war! Fate, in the guise of the dead-letter office, waxes omnipotent and—*voilà!*—the worm turns. Once again, I beg you accept sincerest apologies for the unfortunate carelessness, and I await anxiously your next move.

Enclosed is my forty-fifth move: My knight captures your queen.

Sincerely,
Gossage

Gossage:

Received the letter this morning containing your forty-fifth move (your knight captures my queen?), and also your lengthy explanation regarding the mid-September ellipsis in our correspondence. Let me see if I understand you correctly. Your knight, which I removed from the board weeks ago, you now claim should be resting on the king's fourth square, owing to a letter lost in the mail twenty-three moves ago. I was not aware that any such mishap had occurred, and remember distinctly your making a twenty-second move, which I think was your rook to the queen's sixth square, where it was subsequently butchered in a gambit of yours that misfired tragically.

Currently, the king's fourth square is occupied by *my* rook, and as you are knightless, the dead-letter office notwithstanding, I cannot quite understand what piece you are using to capture my queen with. What I think you mean, as most of your pieces are blockaded, is that you request your king be moved to my bishop's fourth square (your only possibility)—an adjustment I have taken the liberty of making and then countering with today's move, my forty-sixth, wherein I capture your queen and put your king in check. Now your letter becomes clearer.

I think now the last remaining moves of the game can be played out with smoothness and alacrity.

Faithfully,
Vardebedian

Vardebedian:

I have just finished perusing your latest note, the one containing a bizarre forty-sixth move dealing with the removal of my queen from a square on which it has not rested for eleven days. Through patient calculation, I think I have hit upon the cause of your confusion and misunderstanding of the existing facts. That your rook rests on the king's fourth square is an impossibility commensurate with two like snowflakes; if you will refer back to the ninth move of the game, you will see clearly that your rook has long been captured. Indeed, it was that same daring sacrificial combination that ripped your center and cost you *both* your rooks. What are they doing on the board now?

I offer for your consideration that what happened is as follows: The intensity of foray and whirlwind exchanges on and about the twenty-second move left you in a state of slight dissociation, and in your anxiety to hold your own at that point you failed to notice that my usual letter was not forthcoming but instead moved your own pieces twice, giving you a somewhat unfair advantage, wouldn't you say? This is over and done with, and to retrace our steps tediously would be difficult, if not impossible. Therefore, I feel the best way to rectify this entire matter is to allow me the opportunity of two consecutive moves at this time. Fair is fair.

First, then, I take your bishop with my pawn. Then, as this leaves your queen unprotected, I capture her also. I think we can now proceed wtih the last stages unhampered.

Sincerely,
Gossage

P.S.: I am enclosing a diagram showing exactly how the board looks, for your edification in your closing play. As you can see, your king is trapped, unguarded and alone in the center. Best to you.

G.

Gossage:

Received your latest letter today, and while it was just shy of coherence, I think I can see where your bewilderment lies. From your enclosed diagram, it has become apparent to me that for the past six weeks we have been playing two completely different chess games —myself according to our correspondence, you more in keeping with the world as you would have it, rather than with any rational system of order. The knight move which allegedly got lost in the mail would have been impossible on the twenty-second move, as the piece was then standing on the edge of the last file, and the move you describe would have brought it to rest on the coffee table, next to the board.

As for granting you two consecutive moves to make up for one allegedly lost in the mail—surely you jest, Pops. I will honor your first move (you may take my bishop), but I cannot allow the second, and as it is now my turn, I retaliate by removing your queen with my rook. The fact that you tell me I have no rooks means little in actuality, as I need only glance downward at the board to see them darting about with cunning and vigor.

Finally, that diagram of what you fantasize the board to look like indicates a freewheeling, Marx Brothers approach to the game, and, while amusing, this hardly speaks well for your assimilation of *Nimzowitsch on Chess*, which you hustled from the library under your alpaca sweater last winter, because I saw you. I suggest you study the diagram I enclose and rearrange your board accordingly, that we might finish up with some degree of precision.

> Hopefully,
> Vardebedian

Vardebedian:

Not wanting to protract an already disoriented business (I know your recent illness has left your usually hardy constitution somewhat fragmented and disorganized, causing a mild breach with the real world as we know it), I must take this opportunity to undo our sordid tangle of circumstances before it progresses irrevocably to a Kafkaesque conclusion.

Had I realized you were not gentleman enough to allow me an equalizing second move, I would not, on my forty-sixth move, have permitted my pawn to capture your bishop. According to your own diagram, in fact, these two pieces were so placed as to render that impossible, bound as we are to rules established by the World Chess Federation and not the New York State Boxing Commission. Without doubting that your intent was constructive in removing my queen, I interject that only disaster can ensue when you arrogate to yourself this arbitrary power of decision and begin to play dictator,

masking tactical blunders with duplicity and aggression
—a habit you decried in our world leaders several
months ago in your paper on "De Sade and Non-
Violence."

Unfortunately, the game having gone on non-stop, I
have not been able to calculate exactly on which square
you ought to replace the purloined knight, and I suggest we leave it to the gods by having me close my eyes
and toss it back on the board, agreeing to accept whatever spot it may land on. It should add an element of
spice to our little encounter. My forty-seventh move:
My rook captures your knight.

Sincerely,

Gossage

Gossage:

How curious your last letter was! Well-intended, con-
cise, containing all the elements that would appear to
make up what passes among certain reference groups as
a communicative effect, yet tinged throughout by what
Jean-Paul Sartre is so fond of referring to as "nothingness." One is immediately struck by a profound sense
of despair, and reminded vividly of the diaries sometimes left by doomed explorers lost at the Pole, or the
letters of German soldiers at Stalingrad. Fascinating
how the senses disintegrate when faced with an occasional black truth, and scamper amuck, substantiating
mirage and constructing a precarious buffer against the
onslaught of all too terrifying existence!

Be that as it may, my friend, I have just spent the
better part of a week sorting out the miasma of lunatic
alibis known as your correspondence in an effort to ad-
just matters, that our game may be finished simply
once and for all. Your queen is gone. Kiss it off. So are

both your rooks. Forget about one bishop altogether, because I took it. The other is so impotently placed away from the main action of the game that don't count on it or it'll break your heart.

As regards the knight you lost squarely but refuse to give up, I have replaced it at the only conceivable position it could appear, thus granting you the most incredible brace of unorthodoxies since the Persians whipped up this little diversion way back when. It lies at my bishop's seventh square, and if you can pull your ebbing faculties together long enough to appraise the board you will notice this same coveted piece now blocks your king's only means of escape from my suffocating pincer. How fitting that your greedy plot be turned to my advantage! The knight, grovelling its way back into play, torpedoes your end game!

My move is queen to knight five, and I predict mate in one move.

Cordially.
Vardebedian

Vardebedian:

Obviously the constant tension incurred defending a series of numbingly hopeless chess positions has rendered the delicate machinery of your psychic apparatus sluggish, leaving its grasp of external phenomena a jot flimsy. You give me no alternative but to end the contest swiftly and mercifully, removing the pressure before it leaves you permanently damaged.

Knight—yes, knight!—to queen six. Check.

Gossage

Gossage:

Bishop to queen five. Checkmate.

Sorry the competition proved too much for you, but if it's any consolation, several local chess masters have, upon observing my technique, flipped out. Should you want a rematch, I suggest we try Scrabble, a relatively new interest of mine, and one that I might conceivably not run away with so easily.

Vardebedian

Vardebedian:

Rook to knight eight. Checkmate.

Rather than torment you with the further details of my mate, as I believe you are basically a decent man (one day, some form of therapy will bear me out), I accept your invitation to Scrabble in good spirits. Get out your set. Since you played white in chess and thereby enjoyed the advantage of the first move (had I known your limitations, I would have spotted you more), I shall make the first play. The seven letters I have just turned up are O, A, E, J, N, R, and Z—an unpromising jumble that should guarantee, even to the most suspicious, the integrity of my draw. Fortunately, however, an extensive vocabulary, coupled with a penchant for esoterica, has enabled me to bring etymological order out of what, to one less literate, might seem a mishmash. My first word is "ZANJERO." Look it up. Now lay it out, horizontally, the E resting on the center square. Count carefully, not overlooking the double word score for an opening move and the fifty-point bonus for my use of all seven letters. The score is now 116–0.

Your move.

Gossage

Notes from the Overfed

(After reading Dostoevski and the new "Weight Watchers" magazine on the same plane trip)

I am fat. I am disgustingly fat. I am the fattest human I know. I have nothing but excess poundage all over my body. My fingers are fat. My wrists are fat. My eyes are fat. (Can you imagine fat eyes?) I am hundreds of pounds overweight. Flesh drips from me like hot fudge off a sundae. My girth has been an object of disbelief to everyone who's seen me. There is no question about it, I'm a regular fatty. Now, the reader may ask, are there advantages or disadvantages to being built like a planet? I do not mean to be facetious or speak in paradoxes, but I must answer that fat in itself is above bourgeois morality. It is simply fat. That fat could have a value of its own, that fat could be, say, evil or pitying, is, of course, a joke. Absurd! For what is fat after all but an accumulation of pounds? And what are pounds? Simply an aggregate composite of cells. Can a cell be moral? Is a cell beyond good or evil? Who knows—they're so small. No, my friend, we must never attempt to distinguish between good fat and bad fat. We must train ourselves to confront the obese without judging, without thinking this man's fat is first-rate fat and this poor wretch's is grubby fat.

Take the case of K. This fellow was porcine to such a degree that he could not fit through the average door-

frame without the aid of a crowbar. Indeed, K. would
not think to pass from room to room in a conventional
dwelling without first stripping completely and then but-
tering himself. I am no stranger to the insults K. must
have borne from passing gangs of young rowdies. How
frequently he must have been stung by cries of "Tubby!"
and "Blimp!" How it must have hurt when the governor
of the province turned to him on the Eve of Michaelmas
and said, before many dignitaries, "You hulking pot
of *kasha*!"

Then one day, when K. could stand it no longer, he
dieted. Yes, dieted! First sweets went. Then bread, alco-
hol, starches, sauces. In short, K. gave up the very stuff
that makes a man unable to tie his shoelaces without
help from the Santini Brothers. Gradually he began to
slim down. Rolls of flesh fell from his arms and legs.
Where once he looked roly-poly, he suddenly appeared
in public with a normal build. Yes, even an attractive
build. He seemed the happiest of men. I say "seemed,"
for eighteen years later, when he was near death and
fever raged throughout his slender frame, he was heard
to cry out, "My fat! Bring me my fat! Oh, please! I
must have my fat! Oh, somebody lay some avoirdupois
on me! What a fool I've been. To part with one's fat! I
must have been in league with the Devil!" I think that
the point of the story is obvious.

Now the reader is probably thinking, Why, then, if
you are Lard City, have you not joined a circus? Because—and I confess this with no small embarrassment
—I cannot leave the house. I cannot go out because I
cannot get my pants on. My legs are too thick to dress.
They are the living result of more corned beef than
there is on Second Avenue—I would say about twelve
thousand sandwiches per leg. And not all lean, even
though I specified. One thing is certain: If my fat could

speak, it would probably speak of man's intense loneliness—with, oh, perhaps a few additional pointers on how to make a sailboat out of paper. Every pound on my body wants to be heard from, as do Chins Four through Twelve inclusive. My fat is strange fat. It has seen much. My calves alone have lived a lifetime. Mine is not happy fat, but it is real fat. It is not fake fat. Fake fat is the worst fat you can have, although I don't know if the stores still carry it.

But let me tell you how it was that I became fat. For I was not always fat. It is the Church that has made me thus. At one time I was thin—quite thin. So thin, in fact, that to call me fat would have been an error in perception. I remained thin until one day—I think it was my twentieth birthday—when I was having tea and cracknels with my uncle at a fine restaurant. Suddenly my uncle put a question to me. "Do you believe in God?" he asked. "And if so, what do you think He weighs?" So saying, he took a long and luxurious draw on his cigar and, in that confident, assured manner he has cultivated, lapsed into a coughing fit so violent I thought he would hemorrhage.

"I do not believe in God," I told him. "For if there is a God, then tell me, Uncle, why is there poverty and baldness? Why do some men go through life immune to a thousand mortal enemies of the race, while others get a migraine that lasts for weeks? Why are our days numbered and not, say, lettered? Answer me, Uncle. Or have I shocked you?"

I knew I was safe in saying this, because nothing ever shocked the man. Indeed, he had seen his chess tutor's mother raped by Turks and would have found the whole incident amusing had it not taken so much time.

"Good nephew," he said, "there is a God, despite

what you think, and He is everywhere. Yes! Everywhere!"

"Everywhere, Uncle? How can you say that when you don't even know for sure if we exist? True, I am touching your wart at this moment, but could that not be an illusion? Could not all life be an illusion? Indeed, are there not certain sects of holy men in the East who are convinced that *nothing* exists outside their minds except for the Oyster Bar at Grand Central Station? Could it not be simply that we are alone and aimless, doomed to wander in an indifferent universe, with no hope of salvation, nor any prospect except misery, death, and the empty reality of eternal nothing?"

I could see that I made a deep impression on my uncle with this, for he said to me, "You wonder why you're not invited to more parties! Jesus, you're morbid!" He accused me of being nihilistic and then said, in that cryptic way the senile have, "God is not always where one seeks Him, but I assure you, dear nephew, He is everywhere. In these cracknels, for instance." With that, he departed, leaving me his blessing and a check that read like the tab for an aircraft carrier.

I returned home wondering what it was he meant by that one simple statement "He is everywhere. In these cracknels, for instance." Drowsy by then, and out of sorts, I lay down on my bed and took a brief nap. In that time, I had a dream that was to change my life forever. In the dream, I am strolling in the country, when I suddenly notice I am hungry. Starved, if you will. I come upon a restaurant and I enter. I order the open-hot-roast-beef sandwich and a side of French. The waitress, who resembles my landlady (a thoroughly insipid woman who reminds one instantly of some of the hairier lichens), tries to tempt me into ordering the

chicken salad, which doesn't look fresh. As I am con-
versing with this woman, she turns into a twenty-four-
piece started set of silverware. I become hysterical with
laughter, which suddenly turns to tears and then into a
serious ear infection. The room is suffused with a radi-
ant glow, and I see a shimmering figure approach on a
white steed. It is my podiatrist, and I fall to the ground
with guilt.

Such was my dream. I awoke with a tremendous
sense of well-being. Suddenly I was optimistic. Everything was clear. My uncle's statement reverberated to
the core of my very existence. I went to the kitchen and
started to eat. I ate everything in sight. Cakes, breads,
cereals, meat, fruits. Succulent chocolates, vegetables in
sauce, wines, fish, creams and noodles, éclairs, and
wursts totalling in excess of sixty thousand dollars. If
God is everywhere, I had concluded, then He is in food.
Therefore, the more I ate the godlier I would become.
Impelled by this new religious fervor, I glutted myself
like a fanatic. In six months, I was the holiest of holies,
with a heart entirely devoted to my prayers and a stomach that crossed the state line by itself. I last saw my
feet one Thursday morning in Vitebsk, although for all
I know they are still down there. I ate and ate and grew
and grew. To reduce would have been the greatest folly.
Even a sin! For when we lose twenty pounds, dear
reader (and I am assuming you are not as large as I),
we may be losing the twenty best pounds we have! We
may be losing the pounds that contain our genius, our
humanity, our love and honesty or, in the case of one
inspector general I knew, just some unsightly flab
around the hips.

Now, I know what you are saying. You are saying
this is in direct contradiction to everything—yes, everything—I put forth before. Suddenly I am attributing to

neuter flesh, values! Yes, and what of it? Because isn't life that very same kind of contradiction? One's opinion of fat can change in the same manner that the seasons change, that our hair changes, that life itself changes. For life is change and fat is life, and fat is also death. Don't you see? Fat is everything! Unless, of course, you're overweight.

A
Twenties
Memory

I first came to Chicago in the twenties, and that was to see a fight. Ernest Hemingway was with me and we both stayed at Jack Dempsey's training camp. Hemingway had just finished two short stories about prize fighting, and while Gertrude Stein and I both thought they were decent, we agreed they still needed much work. I kidded Hemingway about his forthcoming novel and we laughed a lot and had fun and then we put on some boxing gloves and he broke my nose.

That winter, Alice Toklas, Picasso, and myself took a villa in the south of France. I was then working on what I felt was a major American novel but the print was too small and I couldn't get through it.

In the afternoons, Gertrude Stein and I used to go antique hunting in the local shops, and I remember once asking her if she thought I should become a writer. In the typically cryptic way we were all so enchanted with, she said, "No." I took that to mean yes and sailed for Italy the next day. Italy reminded me a great deal of Chicago, particularly Venice, because both cities have canals and the streets abound with statues and cathedrals by the greatest sculptors of the Renaissance.

That month we went to Picasso's studio in Arles, which was then called Rouen or Zurich, until the French renamed it in 1589 under Louis the Vague. (Louis was a sixteenth-century bastard king who was just mean to everybody.) Picasso was then beginning on what was later to be known as his "blue period," but Gertrude Stein and I had coffee with him, and so he began it ten minutes later. It lasted four years, so the ten minutes did not really mean much.

Picasso was a short man who had a funny way of walking by putting one foot in front of the other until he would take what he called "steps." We laughed at his delightful notions, but toward the late 1930s, with fascism on the rise, there was very little to laugh about. Both Gertrude Stein and I examined Picasso's newest works very carefully, and Gertrude Stein was of the opinion that "art, all art, is merely an expression of something." Picasso disagreed and said, "Leave me alone. I was eating." My own feelings were that Picasso was right. He had been eating.

Picasso's studio was so unlike Matisse's, in that, while Picasso's was sloppy, Matisse kept everything in perfect order. Oddly enough, just the reverse was true. In September of that year, Matisse was commissioned to paint an allegory, but with his wife's illness, it remained unpainted and was finally wallpapered instead. I recall these events so perfectly because it was just before the winter that we all lived in that cheap flat in the north of Switzerland where it will occasionally rain and then just as suddenly stop. Juan Gris, the Spanish cubist, had convinced Alice Toklas to pose for a still life and, with his typical abstract conception of objects, began to break her face and body down to its basic geometrical forms until the police came and pulled him off. Gris was provincially Spanish, and Gertrude Stein used to say that only a true Spaniard could behave as he did; that is, he would speak Spanish and sometimes return to his family in Spain. It was really quite marvellous to see.

I remember one afternoon we were sitting at a gay bar in the south of France with our feet comfortably up on stools in the north of France, when Gertrude Stein said, "I'm nauseous." Picasso thought this to be very funny and Matisse and I took it as a cue to leave for Africa. Seven weeks later, in Kenya, we came upon Hemingway. Bronzed and bearded now, he was already beginning to develop that familiar flat prose style about the eyes and mouth. Here, in the unexplored dark continent, Hemingway had braved chapped lips a thousand times.

"What's doing, Ernest?" I asked him. He waxed eloquent on death and adventure as only he could, and when I awoke he had pitched camp and sat around a great fire fixing us all fine derma appetizers. I kidded him about his new beard and we laughed and sipped cognac and then we put on some boxing gloves and he broke my nose.

That year I went to Paris a second time to talk with a thin, nervous European composer with aquiline profile and remarkably quick eyes who would someday be Igor Stravinsky and then, later, his best friend. I stayed at the home of Man and Sting Ray and Salvador Dali joined us for dinner several times and Dali decided to have a one-man show which he did and it was a huge success, as one man showed up and it was a gay and fine French winter.

I remember one night Scott Fitzgerald and his wife returned home from their New Year's Eve party. It was April. They had consumed nothing but champagne for the past three months, and one previous week, in full evening dress, had driven their limousine off a ninety-foot cliff into the ocean on a dare. There was something real about the Fitzgeralds; their values were basic. They were such modest people, and when Grant Wood later convinced them to pose for his "American Gothic" I remember how flattered they were. All through their sittings, Zelda told me, Scott kept dropping the pitchfork.

I became increasingly friendly with Scott in the next few years, and most of our friends believed that he based the protagonist of his latest novel on me and that I had based my life on his previous novel and I finally wound up getting sued by a fictional character.

Scott was having a big discipline problem and, while we all adored Zelda, we agreed that she had an adverse affect on his work, reducing his output from one novel a year to an occasional seafood recipe and a series of commas.

Finally, in 1929, we all went to Spain together, where Hemingway introduced us to Manolete who was sensitive almost to the point of being effeminate. He wore tight toreador pants or sometimes pedal pushers. Manolete was a great, great artist. Had he not become a bullfighter, his grace was such that he could have been a world-famous accountant.

We had great fun in Spain that year and we travelled and wrote and Hemingway took me tuna fishing and I caught four cans and we laughed and Alice Toklas asked me if I was in love with Gertrude Stein because I had dedicated a book of poems to her even though they were T. S. Eliot's and I said, yes, I loved her, but it could never work because she was far too intelligent for me and Alice Toklas agreed and then we put on some boxing gloves and Gertrude Stein broke my nose.

Count Dracula

Somewhere in Transylvania, Dracula the monster lies sleeping in his coffin, waiting for night to fall. As exposure to the sun's rays would surely cause him to perish, he stays protected in the satin-lined chamber bearing his family name in silver. Then the moment of darkness comes, and through some miraculous instinct the fiend emerges from the safety of his hiding place and, assuming the hideous forms of the bat or the wolf, he prowls the countryside, drinking the blood of his victims. Finally, before the first rays of his archenemy, the sun, announce a new day, he hurries back to the safety of his hidden coffin and sleeps, as the cycle begins anew.

Now he starts to stir. The fluttering of his eyelids are a response to some age-old, unexplainable instinct that the sun is nearly down and his time is near. Tonight, he is particularly hungry and as he lies there, fully awake now, in red-lined Inverness cape and tails, waiting to feel with uncanny perception the precise moment of darkness before opening the lid and emerging, he decides who this evening's victims will be. The baker and his wife, he thinks to himself. Succulent, available, and unsuspecting. The thought of the unwary couple whose trust he has carefully cultivated excites his blood lust to a fever pitch, and he can barely hold back these last seconds before climbing out of the coffin to seek his prey.

Suddenly he knows the sun is down. Like an angel of hell, he rises swiftly, and changing into a bat, flies pell-mell to the cottage of his tantalizing victims.

"Why, Count Dracula, what a nice surprise," the baker's wife says, opening the door to admit him. (He has once again assumed human form, as he enters their home, charmingly concealing his rapacious goal.)

"What brings you here so early?" the baker asks.

"Our dinner date," the Count answers. "I hope I haven't made an error. You did invite me for tonight, didn't you?"

"Yes, tonight, but that's not for seven hours."

"Pardon me?" Dracula queries, looking around the room puzzled.

"Or did you come by to watch the eclipse with us?"

"Eclipse?"

"Yes. Today's the total eclipse."

"What?"

"A few moments of darkness from noon until two minutes after. Look out the window."

"Uh-oh—I'm in big trouble."

"Eh?"

"And now if you'll excuse me . . ."

"What, Count Dracula?"

"Must be going—aha—oh, god . . ." Frantically he fumbles for the door knob.

"Going? You just came."

"Yes—but—I think I blew it very badly . . ."

"Count Dracula, you're pale."

"Am I? I need a little fresh air. It was nice seeing you . . ."

"Come. Sit down. We'll have a drink."

"Drink? No, I must run. Er—you're stepping on my cape."

"Sure. Relax. Some wine."

"Wine? Oh no, gave it up—liver and all that, you know. And now I really must buzz off. I just remembered, I left the lights on at my castle—bills'll be enormous . . ."

"Please," the baker says, his arm around the Count in firm friendship. "You're not intruding. Don't be so polite. So you're early."

"Really, I'd like to stay but there's a meeting of old Roumanian Counts across town and I'm responsible for the cold cuts."

"Rush, rush, rush. It's a wonder you don't get a heart attack."

"Yes, right—and now—"

"I'm making Chicken Pilaf tonight," the baker's wife chimes in. "I hope you like it."

"Wonderful, wonderful," the Count says, with a smile, as he pushes her aside into some laundry. Then, opening a closet door by mistake, he walks in. "Christ, where's the goddamn front door?"

"Ach," laughs the baker's wife, "such a funny man, the Count."

"I knew you'd like that," Dracula says, forcing a chuckle, "now get out of my way." At last he opens the front door but time has run out on him.

"Oh, look, Mama," says the baker, "the eclipse must be over. The sun is coming out again."

"Right," says Dracula, slamming the front door. "I've decided to stay. Pull down the window shades quickly—*quickly*! Let's move it!"

"What window shades?" asks the baker.

"There are none, right? Figures. You got a basement in this joint?"

"No," says the wife affably, "I'm always telling Jarslov to build one but he never listens. That's some Jarslov, my husband."

"I'm all choked up. Where's the closet?"

"You did that one already, Count Dracula. Unt Mama and I laughed at it."

"Ach—such a funny man, the Count."

"Look, I'll be in the closet. Knock at seven-thirty." And with that, the Count steps inside the closet and slams the door.

"Hee-hee—he is so funny, Jarslov."

"Oh, Count. Come out of the closet. Stop being a big silly." From inside the closet comes the muffled voice of Dracula.

"Can't—please—take my word for it. Just let me stay here. I'm fine. Really."

"Count Dracula, stop the fooling. We're already helpless with laughter."

"Can I tell you, I love this closet."

"Yes, but . . ."

"I know, I know . . . it seems strange, and yet here I am, having a ball. I was just saying to Mrs. Hess the other day, give me a good closet and I can stand in it for hours. Sweet woman, Mrs. Hess. Fat but sweet . . . Now, why don't you run along and check back with me at sunset. Oh, Ramona, la da da de da da de, Ramona . . ."

Now the Mayor and his wife, Katia, arrive. They are passing by and have decided to pay a call on their good friends, the baker and his wife.

"Hello, Jarslov. I hope Katia and I are not intruding?"

"Of course not, Mr. Mayor. Come out, Count Dracula! We have company!"

"Is the Count here?" asks the Mayor surprised.

"Yes, and you'l never guess where," says the baker's wife.

"It's so rare to see him around this early. In fact I can't ever remember seeing him around in the daytime."

"Well, he's here. Come out, Count Dracula!"

"Where is he?" Katia asks, not knowing whether to laugh or not.

"Come on out now! Let's go!" The baker's wife is getting impatient.

"He's in the closet," says the baker, apologetically.

"Really?" asks the Mayor.

"Let's go," says the baker with mock good humor as he knocks on the closet door. "Enough is enough. The Mayor's here."

"Come on out, Dracula," His Honor shouts, "let's have a drink."

"No, go ahead. I've got some business in here."

"In the closet?"

"Yes, don't let me spoil your day. I can hear what you're saying. I'l join in if I have anything to add."

Everyone looks at one another and shrugs. Wine is poured and they all drink.

"Some eclipse today," the Mayor says, sipping from his glass.

"Yes," the baker agrees. "Incredible."

"Yeah. Thrilling," says a voice from the closet.

"What, Dracula?"

"Nothing, nothing. Let it go."

And so the time passes, until the Mayor can stand it no longer and forcing open the door to the closet, he shouts, "Come on, Dracula. I always thought you were a mature man. Stop this craziness."

The daylight streams in, causing the evil monster to shriek and slowly dissolve to a skeleton and then to dust before the eyes of the four people present. Leaning down to the pile of white ash on the closet floor, the baker's wife shouts, "Does this mean dinner's off tonight?"

A Little Louder, Please

Understand you are dealing with a man who knocked off *Finegans Wake* on the roller coaster at Coney Island, penetrating the abstruse Joycean arcana with ease, despite enough violent lurching to shake loose my silver fillings. Understand also that I am among the select few who spotted instantly in the Museum of Modern Art's impacted Buick that precise interplay of nuance and shading that Odilon Redon could have achieved had he forsaken the delicate ambiguity of pastels and worked with a car press. Also, laddies, as one whose spate of insights first placed *Godot* in proper perspective for the many confused playgoers who milled sluggishly in the lobby during intermission, miffed at ponying up scalper's money for argle-bargle bereft of one up-tune or a single spangled bimbo, I would have to say my rapport with the seven livelies is pretty solid. Add to this the fact that eight radios conducted simultaneously at Town Hall killed me, and that I still occasionally sit in with my own Philco, after hours, in a Harlem basement where we blow some late weather and news, and where once a laconic field hand named Jess, who had never studied in his life, played the closing Dow-Jones averages with great feeling. Real soul stuff. Finally, to lock my case up tight, note that mine is a stock visage at happenings and underground-movie premières, and that I am a frequent contributor to *Sight and Stream*, a cerebral quarterly dedicated to advanced concepts in cinema and fresh-water fishing. If these are not credentials enough to tag me Joe Sensitive, then, brother, I give up. And yet, with this much perception dripping from me, like maple syrup off waffles, I was reminded recently that I possess an Achilles' heel culturewise that runs up my leg to the back of my neck.

It began one day last January when I was standing in McGinnis' Bar on Broadway, engulfing a slab of the world's richest cheesecake and suffering the guilty, cholesterolish hallucination that I could hear my aorta congealing into a hockey puck. Standing next to me was a nerve-shattering blonde, who waxed and waned under a black chemise with enough provocation to induce lycanthropy in a Boy Scout. For the previous fifteen minutes, my "pass the relish" had been the central theme of our relationship, despite several attempts on my part to generate a little action. As it was, she *had* passed the relish, and I was forced to ladle a small amount on my cheesecake as witness to the integrity of my request.

"I understand egg futures are up," I ventured finally, feigning the insouciance of a man who merged corporations as a sideline. Unaware that her stevedore boy friend had entered, with Laurel and Hardy timing, and was standing right behind me, I gave her a lean, hungry look and can remember cracking wise about Krafft-Ebing just before losing consciousness. The next thing I recall was running down the street to avoid the ire of what appeared to be a Sicilian cousin's club bent on avenging the girl's honor. I sought refuge in the cool dark of a newsreel theatre, where a tour de force by Bugs Bunny and three Librium restored my nervous system to its usual timbre. The main feature came on and turned out to be a travelogue on the New Guinea bush—a topic rivalling "Moss Formations" and "How Penguins Live" for my attention span. "Throwbacks," droned the narrator, "living today not a whit differently from man millions of years ago, slay the wild boar [whose standard of living didn't appear to be up perceptibly, either] and sit around the fire at night acting out the day's kill in pantomime." Pantomime. It hit me with sinus-clearing clarity. Here was a chink in my cultural armor—the only chink, to be sure, but one that has plagued me ever since childhood, when a dumbshow production of Gogol's *The Overcoat* eluded my grasp entirely and had me convinced I was simply watching fourteen Russians doing calisthenics. Always, pantomime was a mystery to me—one that I chose to forget about because of the embarrassment it caused me. But here was that failing again and, to my chagrin, just as bad as ever. I did not understand the frenetic gesticulations of the leading New Guinea aborigine any more than I have ever understood Marcel Marceau in any of those little skits that fill multitudes with such unbounded adulation. I writhed in my seat as the amateur jungle thespian mutely titillated his fellow-primitives, finally garnering hefty mitt with money notices from the tribal elders, and then I slunk, dejected, from the theatre.

At home that evening, I became obsessed with my shortcoming. It was cruelly true: despite my canine celerity in other areas of artistic endeavor, all that was needed was one evening of mine to limn me clearly as Markham's hoe man—stolid, stunned, and a brother to the ox in spades. I began to rage impotently, but the back of my thigh tightened and I was forced to sit. After all, I reasoned, what more elemental form of communication is there? Why was this universal art form patent in meaning to all but me? I tried raging impotently again, and this time brought it off, but mine is a quiet neighborhood, and several minutes later two rednecked spokesmen for the Nineteenth Precinct dropped by to inform me that raging impotently could mean a five-hundred-dollar fine, six months' imprisonment, or both. I thanked them and made a beeline for the sheets, where my struggle to sleep off my monstrous imperfection resulted in eight hours of nocturnal anxiety I wouldn't wish on Macbeth.

A further bone-chilling example of my mimetic short-comings materialized only a few weeks later, when two free tickets to the theatre turned up at my door—the result of my correctly identifying the singing voice of Mama Yancey on a radio program a fortnight prior. First prize was a Bentley, and in my excitement to get my call in to the disc jockey promptly I had bolted naked from the tub. Seizing the telephone with one wet hand while attempting to turn off the radio with the other, I ricocheted off the ceiling, while lights dimmed for miles around, as they did when Lepke got the chair. My second orbit around the chandelier was interrupted by the open drawer of a Louis Quinze desk, which I met head on, catching an ormolu mount across the mouth. A florid insignia on my face, which now looked as if it had been stamped by a rococo cookie cutter, plus a knot on my head the size of an auk egg, affected my lucidity, causing me to place second to Mrs. Sleet Mazursky, and, scotching my dreams of the Bentley, I settled for a pair of freebees to an evening of Off Broadway theatrics. That a famed international pantomimist was on the bill cooled my ardor to the temperature of a polar cap, but, hoping to break the jinx, I decided to attend. I was unable to get a date on only six weeks' notice, so I used the extra ticket to tip my window-washer, Lars, a lethargic menial with all the sensitivity of the Berlin Wall. At first, he thought the little orange pasteboard was edible, but when I explained that it was good for an evening of pantomime—one of the only spectator events outside of a fire that he could hope to understand—he thanked me profusely.

On the night of the performance, the two of us—I in my opera cape and Lars with his pail—split with aplomb from the confines of a Checker cab and, entering the theatre, strode imperiously to our seats, where I studied the program and learned, with some nervousness, that the curtain-raiser was a little silent entertainment entitled *Going to a Picnic*. It began when a wisp of a man walked onstage in kitchen-white makeup and a tight black leotard. Standard picnic dress—I wore it myself to a picnic in Central Park last year, and, with the exception of a few adolescent malcontents who took it as a signal to re-edit my salients, it went unnoticed. The mime now proceeded to spread a picnic blanket, and, instantly, my old confusion set in. He was either spreading a picnic blanket or milking a small goat. Next, he elaborately removed his shoes, except that I'm not positive they were his shoes, because he drank one of them and mailed the other to Pittsburgh. I say "Pittsburgh," but actually it is hard to mime the concept of Pittsburgh, and as I look back on it, I now think what he was miming was not Pittsburgh at all but a man driving a golf cart through a revolving door—or possibly two men dismantling a printing press. How this pertains to a picnic escapes me. The pantomimist then began sorting an invisible collection of rectangular objects, undoubtedly heavy, like a complete set of the *Encyclopaedia Britannica*, which I suspect he was removing from his picnic basket, although from the way he held them they could also have been the Budapest String Quartet, bound and gagged.

By this time, to the surprise of those sitting next to me, I found myself trying, as usual, to help the mime clarify the details of his scene by guessing aloud exactly what he was doing. "Pillow . . . big pillow. Cushion? *Looks* like cushion . . ." This well-meaning participation often upsets the true lover of silent theatre, and I have noticed a tendency on such occasions for those sitting next to me to express uneasiness in various forms, ranging from significant throat-clearings to a lion's-paw swipe on the back of the head, which I once received from a member of a Manhasset housewives' theatre party. On this occasion, a dowager resembling Ichabod Crane snapped her lorgnette quirtlike across my knuckles, with the admonition "Cool it, stud." Then, warming to me, she explained, with the patiently slow enunciation of one addressing a shell-shocked infantry-man, that the mime was now dealing humorously with the various elements that traditionally confound the picnic-goer—ants, rain, and the always-good-for-a-laugh forgotten bottle opener. Temporarily enlightened, I rocked with laughter at the notion of a man harassed by the absence of a bottle opener, and marvelled at its limitless possibilities.

Finally, the mime began blowing glass. Either blow-ing glass or tattooing the student body of Northwestern University. It seemed like the student body of North-western University, but it could have been the men's choir—or a diathermy machine—or any large, extinct quadruped, often amphibious and usually herbivorous, the fossilized remains of which have been found as far north as the Arctic. By now, the audience was doubled up with laughter over the hijinks on the stage. Even the obtuse Lars was wiping tears of joy from his face with his squeegee. But for me it was hopeless; the more I tried, the less I understood. A defeated weariness stole over me, and I slipped off my loafers and called it a day. The next thing I knew, a couple of charwomen at work in the balcony were batting around the pros and cons of bursitis. Gathering my senses by the dim glow of the theatre work light, I straightened my tie and departed for Riker's, where a hamburger and a chocolate malted gave me no trouble whatever as to their meaning, and, for the first time that evening, I threw off my guilty burden. To this day, I remain incomplete culturally, but I'm working on it. If you ever see an aesthete at a pantomime squinting, writhing, and muttering to himself, come up and say hello—but catch me early in the performance; I don't like to be bothered once I'm asleep.

Conversations with Helmholtz

The following are a few samples of conversations taken from the soon-to-be-published book *Conversations with Helmholtz*.

Dr. Helmholtz, now nearing ninety, was a contemporary of Freud's, a pioneer in psychoanalysis, and founder of the school of psychology that bears his name. He is perhaps best known for his experiments in behavior, in which he proved that death is an acquired trait.

Helmholtz resides on a country estate in Lausanne, Switzerland, with his manservant, Hrolf, and his Great Dane, Hrolf. He spends most of his time writing, and is currently revising his autobiography to include himself. The "conversations" were held over a period of several months between Helmholtz and his student and disciple, Fears Hoffnung, whom Helmholtz loathes beyond description but tolerates because he brings him nougat. Their talks covered a variety of subjects, from psychopathology and religion to why Helmholtz can't seem to get a credit card. "The Master," as Hoffnung calls him, emerges as a warm and perceptive human being who maintains he would gladly trade the accomplishments of a lifetime if he could only get rid of his rash.

April 1: Arrived at the Helmholtz house at precisely
10:00 A.M. and was told by the maid that the doctor
was in his room sorting some mail. In my anxiety, I
thought she said the doctor was in his room sorting
some meal. As it turned out, I had heard correctly and
Helmholtz was sorting some meal. He had large fistfuls
of grain in each hand and was arranging it in random
piles. When queried about this he said, "Ach—if only
more people sorted meal." His answer puzzled me, but
I thought it best not to pursue the matter. As he reclined
in his leather chair, I asked him about the early days of
psychoanalysis.

"When I first met Freud, I was already at work on
my theories. Freud was in a bakery. He was attempting
to buy some *Schnecken*, but could not bear to ask for
them by name. Freud was too embarrassed to say the
word '*Schnecken*,' as you probably know. 'Let me have
some of those little cakes,' he would say, pointing to
them. The baker said, 'You mean these *Schnecken*, Herr
Professor?' At that, Freud flushed crimson and fled out
the door muttering, 'Er, no—nothing—never mind.' I
purchased the pastries effortlessly and brought them to
Freud as a gift. We became good friends. I have thought
ever since, certain people are ashamed to say certain
words. Are there any words that embarrass you?"

I explained to Dr. Helmholtz that I could not order
the Lobstermato (a tomato stuffed with lobster) in a
certain restaurant. Helmholtz found that a particularly
asinine word and wished he could scratch the face of
the man who conceived it.

Talk turned back to Freud, who seems to dominate
Helmholtz's every thought, although the two men hated
each other after an argument over some parsley.

"I remember one case of Freud's. Edna S. Hysterical

paralysis of the nose. Could not imitate a bunny when called upon to do so. This caused her great anxiety amongst her friends, who were often cruel. 'Come, Liebchen, show us how you make like a bunny.' Then they'd wiggle their nostrils freely, much to the amusement of each other.

"Freud had her to his office for a series of analytic sessions, but something went amiss and instead of achieving transference to Freud, she achieved transference to his coat tree, a tall wooden piece of furniture across the room. Freud became panicky, as in those days psychoanalysis was regarded skeptically, and when the girl ran off on a cruise with the coat tree Freud swore he'd never practice again. Indeed, for a while, he toyed seriously with the idea of becoming an acrobat, until Ferenczi convinced him he'd never learn to tumble really well."

I could see Helmholtz was getting drowsy now, as he had slid from his chair to the floor under the table, where he lay asleep. Not wishing to press his kindness, I tiptoed out.

April 5: Arrived to find Helmholtz practicing his violin. (He is a marvellous amateur violinist, although he cannot read music and can play only one note.) Again, Helmholtz discussed some of the problems of early psychoanalysis.

"Everyone curried favor with Freud. Rank was jealous of Jones. Jones envied Brill. Brill was annoyed by Adler's presence so much he hid Adler's porkpie hat. Once Freud had some toffee in his pocket and gave a piece to Jung. Rank was infuriated. He complained to me that Freud was favoring Jung. Particularly in the distribution of sweets. I ignored it, as I did not particu-

larly care for Rank since he had recently referred to my
paper on 'Euphoria in Snails' as 'the zenith of mongo-
loid reasoning.'

"Years later, Rank brought the incident up to me
while we were motoring in the Alps. I reminded him
how foolishly he had acted at the time and he admitted
he had been under unusual strain because his first name,
Otto, was spelled the same forwards or backwards and
this depressed him."

Helmholtz invited me to dinner. We sat at a large oak
table which he claims was a gift from Greta Garbo, although she denies any knowledge of it or of Helmholtz.
A typical Helmholtz dinner consisted of: a large raisin,
generous portions of fatback, and an individual can of
salmon. After dinner there were mints and Helmholtz
brought out his collection of lacquered butterflies, which
caused him to become petulant when he realized they
would not fly.

Later, in the sitting room, Helmholtz and I relaxed
over some cigars. (Helmholtz forgot to light his cigar,
but was drawing so hard it was actually getting smaller.)
We discussed some of the Master's most celebrated
cases.

"There was Joachim B. A man in his mid-forties who
could not enter a room that had a cello in it. What was
worse, once he was in a room with a cello he could not
leave unless asked to do so by a Rothschild. In addition
to that, Joachim B. stuttered. But not when he spoke.
Only when he wrote. If he wrote the word 'but,' for instance, it would appear in his letter 'b-b-b-b-b-but.' He
was much teased about this impediment, and attempted
suicide by trying to suffocate himself inside a large
crepe. I cured him with hypnosis, and he was able to
achieve a normal healthy life, although in later years he

constantly fantasized meeting a horse who advised him to take up architecture."

Helmholtz talked about the notorious rapist, V., who at one time held all London in terror.

"A most unusual case of perversion. He had a recurring sexual fantasy in which he is humiliated by a group of anthropologists and forced to walk around bowlegged, which he confessed gave him great sexual pleasure. He recalled as a child surprising his parents' housekeeper, a woman of loose morals, in the act of kissing some watercress, which he found erotic. As a teen-ager he was punished for varnishing his brother's head, although his father, a house painter by trade, was more upset over the fact he gave the boy only one coat.

"V. attacked his first woman at eighteen, and thereafter raped half a dozen per week for years. The best I was able to do with him in therapy was to substitute a more socially acceptable habit to replace his aggressive tendencies; and thereafter when he chanced upon an unsuspecting female, instead of assaulting her, he would produce a large halibut from his jacket and show it to her. While the sight of it caused consternation in some, the women were spared any violence and some even confessed their lives were immeasurably enriched by the experience."

April 12: This time Helmholtz was not feeling too well. He had gotten lost in a meadow the previous day and fallen down on some pears. He was confined to bed, but sat upright and even laughed when I told him I had an abscess.

We discussed his theory of reverse-psychology, which came to him shortly after Freud's death. (Freud's death, according to Ernest Jones, was the event that caused the

final break between Helmholtz and Freud, and the two
rarely spoke afterwards.)

At the time, Helmholtz had developed an experiment
where he would ring a bell and a team of white mice
would escort Mrs. Helmholtz out the door and deposit
her on the curb. He did many such behavioristic experiments and only stopped when a dog trained to salivate
on cue refused to let him in the house for the holidays.
He is, incidentally, still credited with the classic paper
on "Unmotivated Giggling in Caribou."

"Yes, I founded the school of reverse psychology.
Quite by accident, in fact. My wife and I were both
comfortably tucked in bed when I suddenly desired a
drink of water. Too lazy to get it myself, I asked Mrs.
Helmholtz to get it for me. She refused, saying she was
exhausted from lifting chick peas. We argued over who
should get it. Finally, I said, 'I don't really want a glass
of water anyhow. In fact, a glass of water is the last
thing in the world I want.' At that, the woman sprang
up and said, 'Oh, you don't want any water, eh? That's
too bad.' And she quickly left bed and got me some. I
tried to discuss the incident with Freud at the analysts'
outing in Berlin, but he and Jung were partners in the
three-legged race and were too wrapped up in the fes-
tivities to listen.

"Only years later did I find a way to utilize this principle in the treatment of depression, and was able to
cure the great opera singer, J., of the morbid apprehen-
sion he would one day wind up in a hamper."

April 18: Arrived to find Helmholtz trimming some
rose bushes. He was quite eloquent on the beauty of
flowers, which he loves because "they're not always
borrowing money."

We talked about contemporary psychoanalysis, which

Helmholtz regards as a myth kept alive by the couch industry.

"These modern analysts! They charge so much. In my day, for five marks Freud himself would treat you. For ten marks, he would treat you and press your pants. For fifteen marks, Freud would let *you* treat *him*, and that included a choice of any two vegetables. Thirty dollars an hour! Fifty dollars an hour! The Kaiser only got twelve and a quarter for being Kaiser! And he had to walk to work! And the length of treatment! Two years! Five years! If one of us couldn't cure a patient in six months we would refund his money, take him to any musical revue and he would receive either a mahogany fruit bowl or a set of stainless steel carving knives. I remember you could always tell the patients Jung failed with, as he would give them large stuffed pandas."

We strolled along the garden path and Helmholtz turned to other subjects of interest. He was a veritable spate of insights and I managed to preserve some by jotting them down.

On the human condition: "If man were immortal, do you realize what his meat bills would be?"

On religion: "I don't believe in an afterlife, although I am bringing a change of underwear."

On literature: "All literature is a footnote to Faust. I have no idea what I mean by that."

I am convinced Helmholtz is a very great man.

Viva Vargas!
Excerpts from the Diary of a Revolutionary

June 3: Viva Vargas! Today we took to the hills. Outraged and disgusted at the exploitation of our little country by the corrupt Arroyo régime, we sent Julio to the place with a list of our grievances and demands, none hastily arrived at nor, in my opinion, excessive. As it turned out, Arroyo's busy schedule did not include taking time away from being fanned to meet with our beloved rebel emissary, and instead he referred the entire matter to his minister, who said he would give our petitions his full consideration, but first he just wanted to see how long Julio could smile with his head under molten lava.

Because of many indignations such as this one, we have at last, behind the inspired leadership of Emilio Molina Vargas, decided to take matters into our own hands. If this be treason, we yelled on street corners, let us make the most of it.

I was, unfortunately, lolling in a hot tub when word arrived that the police would be by shortly to hang me. Bounding from my bath with understandable alacrity, I stepped on a wet bar of soap and cascaded off the front patio, luckily breaking the fall with my teeth, which skidded around the ground like loose Chiclets. Though naked and bruised, survival dictated I act quickly, and mounting El Diablo, my stallion, I gave the rebel yell! The horse reared and I slid down his back to the ground, fracturing certain small bones.

Were all this not devastating enough, I scarcely got twenty feet by foot when I remembered my printing press, and not wanting to leave behind such a potent political weapon or piece of evidence, I doubled back to retrieve it. As luck would have it, the thing weighed more than it looked, and lifting it was a job more suited to a derrick than a hundred-and-ten-pound college student. When the police arrived, my hand was caught in the machinery as it roared uncontrollably, reprinting large passages of Marx down my bare back. Don't ask me how I managed to tear loose and vault out a back window. Luckily I eluded the police and made my way to safety in Vargas' camp.

June 4: How peaceful it is here in the hills. Living out under the stars. A group of dedicated men all working toward a common goal. Although I had anticipated a say in the actual planning of the campaigns, Vargas felt my services might better be employed as company cook. This is not an easy job with foodstuffs scarce, but somebody has to do it and, all things considered, my first meal was a big hit. True, not all the men are terribly partial to Gila monster but we can't be choosy, and apart from some picayune eaters who are prejudiced against any reptile, dinner came off without incident.

I overheard Vargas today and he is quite sanguine about our prospects. He feels we will gain control of the capital sometime in December. His brother, Luis, on the other hand, an introspective man by nature, feels it is only a question of time before we starve to death. The Vargas brothers constantly bicker over military strategy and political philosophy, and it is hard to imagine that these two great rebel chieftains were only last week a couple of men's room attendants at the local Hilton. Meanwhile, we wait.

June 10: Spent the day drilling. How miraculously we are being changed from a scruffy band of guerrillas to a hard-core army. This morning Hernandez and I practiced using machetes, our razor-sharp sugar-cane knives, and due to a burst of overzealousness by my partner, I found out I had type-O blood. The worst thing is the waiting. Arturo has a guitar but can only play "Cielito Lindo," and while the men rather liked to hear it at first, he seldom gets any more requests for it. I tried preparing the Gila monster a new way and I think the men enjoyed it, although I noticed some had to chew hard and snap their heads back to get it down.

I overheard Vargas again today. He and his brother were discussing their plans after we take the capital. I wonder what post he is saving for me when the revolution is completed. I am quite confident my fierce loyalty, which can only be described as canine, will pay off.

July 1: A party of our best men raided a village for food today, and got a chance to employ many of the tactics we have been working on. Most of the rebels acquitted themselves nicely, and even though the group was slaughtered, Vargas considers it a moral victory. Those of us who were not in on the raid sat around camp while Arturo favored us with some "Cielito Lindo." Morale remains high, even though food and arms are virtually nonexistent and time passes slowly. Luckily we are distracted by the hundred-degree heat, which I think accounts for much of the funny gurgling noise the men make. Our time will come.

July 10: Today was generally a good day, despite the

fact that we were ambushed by Arroyo's men and badly decimated. This was partially my fault as I gave away our position by inadvertently shrieking the names of the Christian triumvirate when a tarantula crawled over my leg. For several moments I could not dislodge the tenacious little spider as it made its way into the inner recesses of my garments, causing me to gyrate spastically toward the stream and thrash about in it for what seemed like forty-five minutes. Shortly after, Arroyo's soldiers opened fire on us. We fought gamely, although the shock of being surprised created a mild disorganization, and for the first ten minutes our men were shooting at each other. Vargas narrowly escaped catastrophe as a live hand grenade landed at his feet. He commanded me to fall on it, aware that he alone is indispensable to our cause, and I did so. As providence would have it, the grenade did not explode and I walked away unharmed except for a slight twitch and the inability to fall asleep unless someone holds my hand.

July 15: The morale of the men seems to be holding up, despite certain minor setbacks. First, Miguel stole some ground-to-ground missiles but mistook them for ground-to-air missiles and, attempting to down several of Arroyo's planes, blew all our trucks up. When he tried to laugh it off, José became furious and they fought. Later, they patched things up and deserted. Desertion, incidentally, could become a major problem, although at this moment optimism and team spirit have held it down to three out of every four men. I, of course, remain loyal and do the cooking, but the men still do not seem to appreciate the difficulty of that assignment. The fact is, my life has been threatened if I don't come up with an alternative to Gila monster. Sometimes soldiers can be so unreasonable. Still, perhaps one of these days

I will surprise them with something new. Meanwhile we sit around the camp and wait. Vargas is pacing in his tent and Arturo sits playing "Cielito Lindo."

August 1: Despite all we have to be thankful for, there is no doubt that a certain tension has set in here at rebel headquarters. Little things, apparent only to the observant eye, indicate an undercurrent of uneasiness. For one thing, there are quite a few stabbings among the men, as quarrels become more frequent. Also an attempt to raid an ammunitions depot and rearm ourselves ended in a rout when Jorge's signal flare went off prematurely in his pocket. All the men were chased except for Jorge, who was captured after banging off two dozen buildings like a pinball. Back at camp in the evening, when I brought out the Gila monster the men rioted. Several of them held me down while Ramon struck me with my ladle. I was mercifully saved by an electrical storm that claimed three lives. Finally, with frustrations at a peak, Arturo struck up "Cielito Lindo" and some of the less musically inclined ones in the group took him behind a rock and forced-fed him his guitar.

On the plus side of the ledger, Vargas' diplomatic envoy, after many unsuccessful attempts, managed to conclude an interesting deal with the CIA where, in return for our unswerving fealty toward their policies forever, they are obligated to supply us with no less than fifty barbecued chickens.

Vargas now feels that perhaps he was premature in predicting a December success and indicates that total victory might require additional time. Strangely enough, he has turned from his field maps and charts and relies more heavily now on astrological readings and the entrails of birds.

August 12: The situation has taken a turn for the worse. As luck would have it, the mushrooms I so carefully picked to vary the menu with, turned out to be poisonous, and while the only really disconcerting side effect was some minor convulsions most of the men suffered, they seemed unduly embittered. On top of that, the CIA has reconsidered our chances of bringing off the revolution and as a result threw Arroyo and his cabinet a conciliatory brunch at Wolfie's in Miami Beach. This, coupled with a gift of 24 jet bombers, Vargas interprets as a subtle shift in their sympathies.

Morale still seems reasonably high and, while the desertion rate has risen, it is still limited to those who can walk. Vargas himself appears to be a bit morose and has taken to saving string. It is now his feeling that life under the Arroyo régime might not be all that uncomfortable, and he wonders if we should not reorient the men that are left, abandon the ideals of the revolution, and form a rhumba band. Meanwhile the heavy rains have caused the mountain to landslide, and the Juarez brothers were carried off into the gorge as they slept. We have dispatched an emissary to Arroyo, with a modified list of our demands, taking care to strike out the portions concerning his unconditional surrender and substituting in its place an award-winning recipe for guacamole. I wonder how it will all turn out.

August 15: We have taken the capital! The incredible details follow:

After much deliberation, the men took a vote and decided to pin our last hopes on a suicide mission, guessing that the element of surprise might be just the thing to offset Arroyo's superior forces. As we marched through the jungle, towards the palace, hunger and fatigue slowly sapped a portion of our resolve and, ap-

proaching our destination, we decided to switch tactics
and see if grovelling would work. We turned ourselves
over to the palace guards, who brought us at gunpoint
before Arroyo. The dictator took into consideration the
mitigating fact that we had given up voluntarily, and
while he still planned to disembowel Vargas, the rest of
us were going to get off with being skinned alive. Re-
ëvaluating our situation in light of this fresh concept,
we succumbed to panic and bolted in all directions
while the guards opened fire. Vargas and I raced up-
stairs and, seeking a place to hide, burst into Madame
Arroyo's boudoir, surprising her in a moment of illicit
passion with Arroyo's brother. Both became flustered.
Arroyo's brother then drew his revolver and let fly a
shot. Unbeknownst to him, this acted as a signal to a
group of mercenaries who had been hired by the CIA
to help clean us out of the hills in return for Arroyo's
granting the United States rights to open Orange Julius
stands here. The mercenaries, who were themselves confused regarding their loyalties due to weeks of American foreign policy equivocating, attacked the palace by
mistake. Arroyo and his staff suddenly suspected a CIA
double cross and turned their guns on the invaders.
Concurrently a long-smoldering plot to assassinate Arroyo by several Maoists misfired when a bomb they
planted in a taco went off prematurely, exorcising the
left wing of the palace and projecting Arroyo's wife and
brother through some wood beams.

Grabbing a valise of Swiss bankbooks, Arroyo made
for the rear door and his ever-ready Lear jet. His pilot
took off amidst a volley of gunfire but, confused by the
hectic events of the moment, threw the wrong switch,
sending the plane into a nose dive. Moments later, it
crashed into the mercenary army camp, laying their
ranks waste and causing them to give up.

Throughout this, Vargas, our beloved leader, brilliantly adopted a policy of watchful waiting, which he executed by crouching motionless at the fireplace and assuming the disguise of a decorative blackamoor. As the coast became clear he advanced on tiptoe to the central office and assumed power, pausing only to open the royal refrigerator and slap together a deviled ham sandwich.

We celebrated all through the night and everyone got very drunk. I spoke with Vargas afterwards about the serious business of running a country. While he believes free elections are essential to any democracy, he prefers to wait until the people become a bit more educated before there is any voting. Until then, he has improvised a workable system of government based on divine monarchy and has rewarded my loyalty by allowing me to sit by his right hand at mealtime. Plus I also am responsible for seeing the latrine is spotless.

The Discovery and Use of the Fake Ink Blot

There is no evidence of a fake ink blot appearing anywhere in the West before the year 1921, although Napoleon was known to have had great fun with the joy buzzer, a device concealed in the palm of the hand causing an electric-like vibration upon contact. Napoleon would offer the regal hand in friendship to a foreign dignitary, buzz the unsuspecting victim's palm and roar with imperial laughter as the redfaced dupe did an improvised jig to the delight of the court.

The joy buzzer underwent many modifications, the most celebrated of which occurred after the introduction of chewing gum by Santa Anna (I believe chewing gum was originally a dish of his wife's that simply would not go down) and took the form of a spearmint-gum pack equipped with a subtle mousetrap mechanism. The sucker, offered a fresh stick, experienced a piercing sting as the iron bar came springing down on his naive fingertips. The first reaction was generally one of pain, then contagious laughter, and finally a kind of folk wisdom. It is no secret that the snappy-chewing-gum gag lightened matters at the Alamo considerably; and although there were no survivors, most observers feel things could have gone substantially worse without this cunning little gimmick.

With the advent of the Civil War, Americans turned more and more to escaping the horrors of a disintegrating nation; and while the Northern generals preferred amusing themselves with the dribble glass, Robert E. Lee passed many a crucial moment with his brilliant use of the squirt flower. In the early part of the War, no one ever came away from smelling the apparent "lovely carnation" in Lee's lapel without getting a generous eyeful of Suwanee River water. As things went badly for the South, however, Lee abandoned the once-fashionable artifice and relied simply on placing a carpet tack on the chair seats of people whom he did not like.

After the War and right up to the early 1900s and the so-called era of the robber barons, sneezing powder and a little tin can marked ALMONDS, wherefrom several huge spring serpents would leap into the victim's face, provided all that was worthy in the area of tomfoolery. It is said J. P. Morgan preferred the former, while the elder Rockefeller felt more at home with the latter.

Then, in 1921, a group of biologists meeting in Hong Kong to buy suits discovered the fake ink blot. It had long been a staple of the Oriental repertoire of diversions, and several of the later dynasties retained power by their brilliant manipulation of what appeared to be a spilled bottle and an ugly inkstain, but was in reality a tin blot.

The first ink blots, it was learned, were crude, constructed to eleven feet in diameter and fooled nobody.

However, with the discovery of the concept of smaller sizes by a Swiss physicist, who proved that an object of a particular size could be reduced in size simply by "making it smaller," the fake ink blot came into its own.

It remained in its own until 1934, when Franklin Delano Roosevelt removed it from its own and placed it in someone else's. Roosevelt utilized it cleverly to settle a strike in Pennsylvania, the details of which are amusing. Embarrassed leaders of both labor and management were convinced that a bottle of ink had been spilled, ruining someone's priceless Empire sofa. Imagine how relieved they were to learn it was all in fun. Three days later the steel mills were reopened.

Mr. Big

I was sitting in my office, cleaning the debris out of my thirty-eight and wondering where my next case was coming from. I like being a private eye, and even though once in a while I've had my gums massaged with an automobile jack, the sweet smell of greenbacks makes it all worth it. Not to mention the dames, which are a minor preoccupation of mine that I rank just ahead of breathing. That's why, when the door to my office swung open and a long-haired blonde named Heather Butkiss came striding in and told me she was a nudie model and needed my help, my salivary glands shifted into third. She wore a short skirt and a tight sweater and her figure described a set of parabolas that could cause cardiac arrest in a yak.

"What can I do for you, sugar?"

"I want you to find someone for me."

"Missing person? Have you tried the police?"

"Not exactly, Mr. Lupowitz."

"Call me Kaiser, sugar. All right, so what's the scam?"

"God."

"God?"

"That's right, God. The Creator, the Underlying Principle, the First Cause of Things, the All Encompassing. I want you to find Him for me."

I've had some fruit cakes up in the office before, but
when they're built like she was, you listened.

"Why?"

"That's my business, Kaiser. You just find Him."

"I'm sorry, sugar. You got the wrong boy."

"But why?"

"Unless I know all the facts," I said, rising.

"O.K., O.K.," she said, biting her lower lip. She
straightened the seam of her stocking, which was strictly
for my benefit, but I wasn't buying any at the moment.

"Let's have it on the line, sugar."

"Well, the truth is—I'm not really a nudie model."

"No?"

"No. My name is not Heather Butkiss, either. It's
Claire Rosensweig and I'm a student at Vassar. Philosophy major. History of Western Thought and all that. I
have a paper due January. On Western religion. All the
other kids in the course will hand in speculative papers.
But I want to *know*. Professor Grebanier said if anyone
finds out for sure, they're a cinch to pass the course.
And my dad's promised me a Mercedes if I get straight
A's."

I opened a deck of Luckies and a pack of gum and
had one of each. Her story was beginning to interest
me. Spoiled coed. High IQ and a body I wanted to
know better.

"What does God look like?"

"I've never seen him."

"Well, how do you know He exists?"

"That's for you to find out."

"Oh, great. Then you don't know what he looks like?
Or where to begin looking?"

"No. Not really. Although I suspect he's everywhere.
In the air, in every flower, in you and I—and in this
chair."

"Uh huh." So she was a pantheist. I made a mental note of it and said I'd give her case a try—for a hundred bucks a day, expenses, and a dinner date. She smiled and okayed the deal. We rode down in the elevator together. Outside it was getting dark. Maybe God did exist and maybe He didn't, but somewhere in that city there were sure a lot of guys who were going to try and keep me from finding out.

My first lead was Rabbi Itzhak Wiseman, a local cleric who owed me a favor for finding out who was rubbing pork on his hat. I knew something was wrong when I spoke to him because he was scared. Real scared.

"Of course there's a you-know-what, but I'm not even allowed to say His name or He'll strike me dead, which I could never understand why someone is so touchy about having his name said."

"You ever see Him?"

"Me? Are you kidding? I'm lucky I get to see my grandchildren."

"Then how do you know He exists?"

"How do I know? What kind of question is that? Could I get a suit like this for fourteen dollars if there was no one up there? Here, feel a gabardine—how can you doubt?"

"You got nothing more to go on?"

"Hey—what's the Old Testament? Chopped liver? How do you think Moses got the Israelites out of Egypt? With a smile and a tap dance? Believe me, you don't part the Red Sea with some gismo from Korvette's. It takes power."

"So he's tough, eh?"

"Yes. Very tough. You'd think with all that success he'd be a lot sweeter."

"How come you know so much?"

"Because we're the chosen people. He takes best care of us of all His children, which I'd also like to someday discuss with Him."

"What do you pay Him for being chosen?"

"Don't ask."

So that's how it was. The Jews were into God for a lot. It was the old protection racket. Take care of them in return for a price. And from the way Rabbi Wiseman was talking, He soaked them plenty. I got into a cab and made it over to Danny's Billiards on Tenth Avenue. The manager was a slimy little guy I didn't like.

"Chicago Phil here?"

"Who wants to know?"

I grabbed him by the lapels and took some skin at the same time.

"What, punk?"

"In the back," he said, with a change of attitude.

Chicago Phil. Forger, bank robber, strong-arm man, and avowed atheist.

"The guy never existed, Kaiser. This is the straight dope. It's a big hype. There's no Mr. Big. It's a syndicate. Mostly Sicilian. It's international. But there is no actual head. Except maybe the Pope."

"I want to meet the Pope."

"It can be arranged," he said, winking.

"Does the name Claire Rosensweig mean anything to you?"

"No."

"Heather Butkiss?"

"Oh, wait a minute. Sure. She's that peroxide job with the bazooms from Radcliffe."

"Radcliffe? She told me Vassar."

"Well, she's lying. She's a teacher at Radcliffe. She was mixed up with a philosopher for a while."

"Pantheist?"

"No. Empiricist, as I remember. Bad guy. Completely rejected Hegel or any dialectical methodology."

"One of those."

"Yeah. He used to be a drummer with a jazz trio. Then he got hooked on Logical Positivism. When that didn't work, he tried Pragmatism. Last I heard he stole a lot of money to take a course in Schopenhauer at Columbia. The mob would like to find him—or get their hands on his textbooks so they can resell them."

"Thanks, Phil."

"Take it from me, Kaiser. There's no one out there. It's a void. I couldn't pass all those bad checks or screw society the way I do if for one second I was able to recognize any authentic sense of Being. The universe is strictly phenomenological. Nothing's eternal. It's all meaningless."

"Who won the fifth at Aqueduct?"

"Santa Baby."

I had a beer at O'Rourke's and tried to add it all up, but it made no sense at all. Socrates was a suicide—or so they said. Christ was murdered. Neitzsche went nuts. If there was someone out there, He sure as hell didn't want anybody to know it. And why was Claire Rosensweig lying about Vassar? Could Descartes have been right? Was the universe dualistic? Or did Kant hit it on the head when he postulated the existence of God on moral grounds?

That night I had dinner with Claire. Ten minutes after the check came, we were in the sack and, brother, you can have your Western thought. She went through the kind of gymnastics that would have won first prize in the Tia Juana Olympics. After, she lay on the pillow next to me, her long blond hair sprawling. Our naked bodies still intertwined. I was smoking and staring at the ceiling.

"Claire, what if Kierkegaard's right?"

"You mean?"

"If you can never really *know*. Only have faith."

"That's absurd."

"Don't be so rational."

"Nobody's being rational, Kaiser." She lit a cigarette. "Just don't get ontological. Not now. I couldn't bear it if you were ontological with me."

She was upset. I leaned over and kissed her, and the phone rang. She got it.

"It's for you."

The voice on the other end was Sergeant Reed of Homicide.

"You still looking for God?"

"Yeah."

"An all-power Being? Great Oneness, Creator of the Universe? First Cause of All Things?"

"That's right."

"Somebody with that description just showed up at the morgue. You better get down here right away."

It was Him all right, and from the looks of Him it was a professional job.

"He was dead when they brought Him in."

"Where'd you find Him?"

"A warehouse on Delancey Street."

"Any clues?"

"It's the work of an existentialist. We're sure of that."

"How can you tell?"

"Haphazard way how it was done. Doesn't seem to be any system followed. Impulse."

"A crime of passion?"

"You got it. Which means you're a suspect, Kaiser."

"Why me?"

"Everybody down at headquarters knows how you feel about Jaspers."

"That doesn't make me a killer."

"Not yet, but you're a suspect."

Outside on the street I sucked air into my lungs and tried to clear my head. I took a cab over to Newark and got out and walked a block to Giordino's Italian Restaurant. There, at a back table, was His Holiness. It was the Pope, all right. Sitting with two guys I had seen in half a dozen police line-ups.

"Sit down," he said, looking up from his fettucine. He held out a ring. I gave him my toothiest smile, but didn't kiss it. It bothered him and I was glad. Point for me.

"Would you like some fettucine?"

"No thanks, Holiness. But you go ahead."

"Nothing? Not even a salad?"

"I just ate."

"Suit yourself, but they make a great Roquefort dressing here. Not like the Vatican, where you can't get a decent meal."

"I'll come right to the point, Pontiff. I'm looking for God."

"You came to the right person."

"Then He does exist?" They all found this very amusing and laughed. The hood next to me said, "Oh, that's funny. Bright boy wants to know if He exists."

I shifted my chair to get comfortable and brought the leg down on his little toe. "Sorry." But he was steaming.

"Sure He exists, Lupowitz, but I'm the only one that communicates with Him. He speaks only through me."

"Why you, pal?"

"Because I got the red suit."

"This get-up?"

"Don't knock it. Every morning I rise, put on this red

suit, and suddenly I'm a big cheese. It's all in the suit.
I mean, face it, if I went around in slacks and a sports
jacket, I couldn't get arrested religion-wise."

"Then it's a hype. There's no God."

"I don't know. But what's the difference? The
money's good."

"You ever worry the laundry won't get your red suit
back on time and you'll be like the rest of us?"

"I use the special one-day service. I figure it's worth
the extra few cents to be safe."

"Name Claire Rosensweig mean anything to you?"

"Sure. She's in the science department at Bryn
Mawr."

"Science, you say? Thanks."

"For what?"

"The answer, Pontiff." I grabbed a cab and shot over
the George Washington Bridge. On the way I stopped at
my office and did some fast checking. Driving to Claire's
apartment, I put the pieces together, and for the first
time they fit. When I got there she was in a diaphanous
peignoir and something seemed to be troubling her.

"God is dead. The police were here. They're looking
for you. They think an existentialist did it."

"No, sugar. It was you."

"What? Don't make jokes, Kaiser."

"It was you that did it."

"What are you saying?"

"You, baby. Not Heather Butkiss or Claire Rosensweig, but Doctor Ellen Shepherd."

"How did you know my name?"

"Professor of physics at Bryn Mawr. The youngest
one ever to head a department there. At the mid-winter
Hop you get stuck on a jazz musician who's heavily into
philosophy. He's married, but that doesn't stop you. A
couple of nights in the hay and it feels like love. But it

doesn't work out because something comes between you. God. Y'see, sugar, he believed, or wanted to, but you, with your pretty little scientific mind, had to have absolute certainty."

"No, Kaiser, I swear."

"So you pretend to study philosophy because that gives you a chance to eliminate certain obstacles. You get rid of Socrates easy enough, but Descartes takes over, so you use Spinoza to get rid of Descartes, but when Kant doesn't come through you have to get rid of him too."

"You don't know what you're saying."

"You made mincemeat out of Leibnitz, but that wasn't good enough for you because you knew if anybody believed Pascal you were dead, so he had to be gotten rid of too, but that's where you made your mistake because you trusted Martin Buber. Except, sugar, he was soft. He believed in God, so you had to get rid of God yourself."

"Kaiser, you're mad!"

"No, baby. You posed as a pantheist and that gave you access to Him—*if* He existed, which he did. He went with you to Shelby's party and when Jason wasn't looking, you killed Him."

"Who the hell are Shelby and Jason?"

"What's the difference? Life's absurd now anyway."

"Kaiser," she said, suddenly trembling. "You wouldn't turn me in?"

"Oh yes, baby. When the Supreme Being gets knocked off, *somebody's* got to take the rap."

"Oh, Kaiser, we could go away together. Just the two of us. We could forget about philosophy. Settle down and maybe get into semantics."

"Sorry, sugar. It's no dice."

She was all tears now as she started lowering the

shoulder straps of her peignoir and I was standing there suddenly with a naked Venus whose whole body seemed to be saying, Take me—I'm yours. A Venus whose right hand tousled my hair while her left hand had picked up a forty-five and was holding it behind my back. I let go with a slug from my thirty-eight before she could pull the trigger, and she dropped her gun and doubled over in disbelief.

"How could you, Kaiser?"

She was fading fast, but I managed to get it in, in time.

"The manifestation of the universe as a complex idea unto itself as opposed to being in or outside the true Being of itself is inherently a conceptual nothingness or Nothingness in relation to any abstract form of existing or to exist or having existed in perpetuity and not subject to laws of physicality or motion or ideas relating to non-matter or the lack of objective Being or subjective otherness."

It was a subtle concept but I think she understood before she died.

ABOUT THE AUTHOR
• • • • • • • • • • •

After he was ejected from both New York University and City College, WOODY ALLEN turned to a professional writing career, at first for television and comedians. In 1964 he decided to become a comedian himself.

In addition to his numerous nightclub and television appearances, Mr. Allen has made three comedy record albums of live concert appearances and somehow found time to write two long-running hits for Broadway, *Don't Drink the Water* and *Play It Again, Sam* (the latter starring himself). His first film script, written in 1964, was the enormously popular *What's New Pussycat?* He has also written, directed and starred in six films to date: *Take the Money and Run, Bananas, Everything You Always Wanted to Know About Sex, Sleeper, Love and Death* and *Annie Hall.*

Mr. Allen has written and appeared in his own television specials and is a frequent contributor to *The New Yorker,* among other periodicals.

His one regret in life is that he is not someone else.

VINTAGE BIOGRAPHY AND AUTOBIOGRAPHY

VINTAGE BELLES—LETTRES

VINTAGE FICTION, POETRY, AND PLAYS